Little ★ ★
★ Gabriel

★

Drawn by

Al Kilgore

ABOUT COMICS | Camarillo, California

Little Gabriel
Originally published by Abbey Books, 1958
About Comics edition published August, 2018

Customized editions available

Send all queries to *questions@aboutcomics.com*

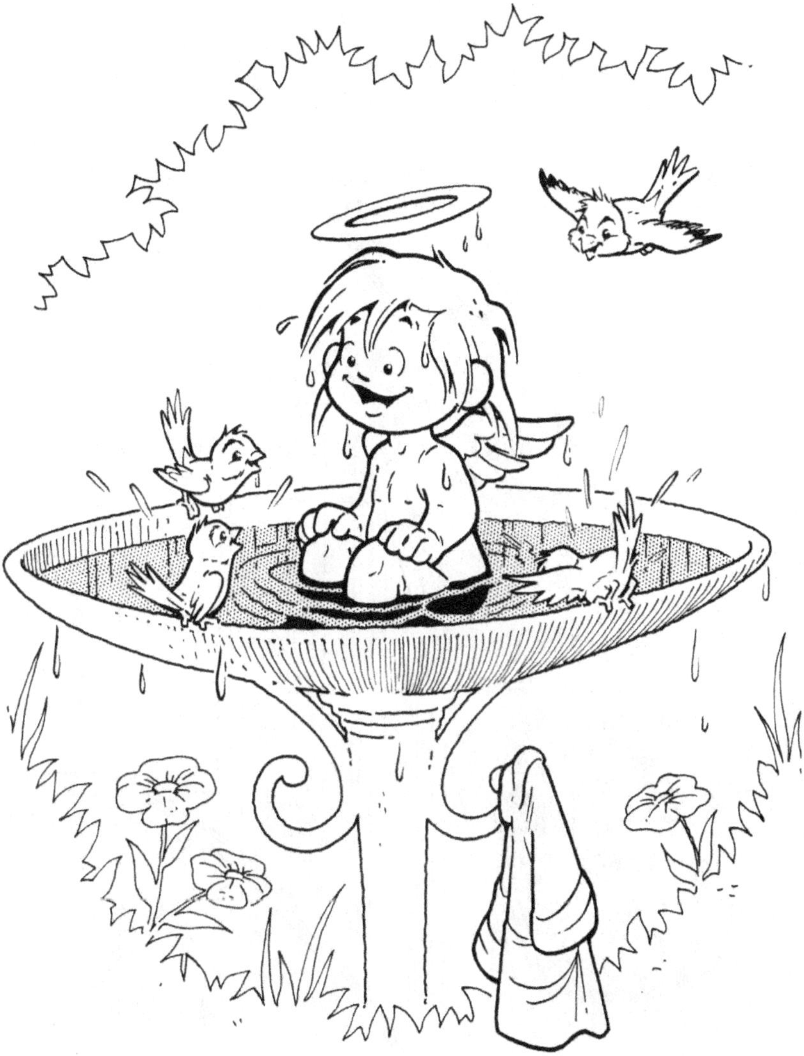

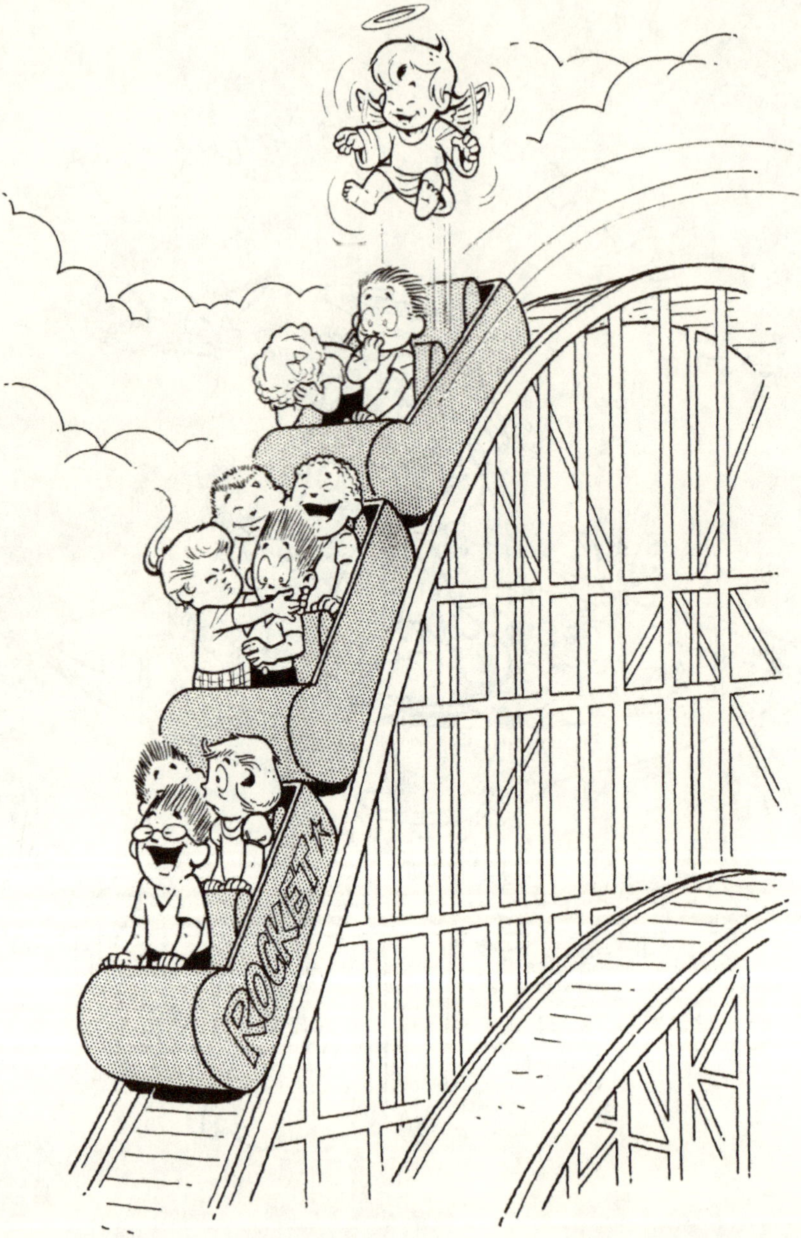
ROCKET

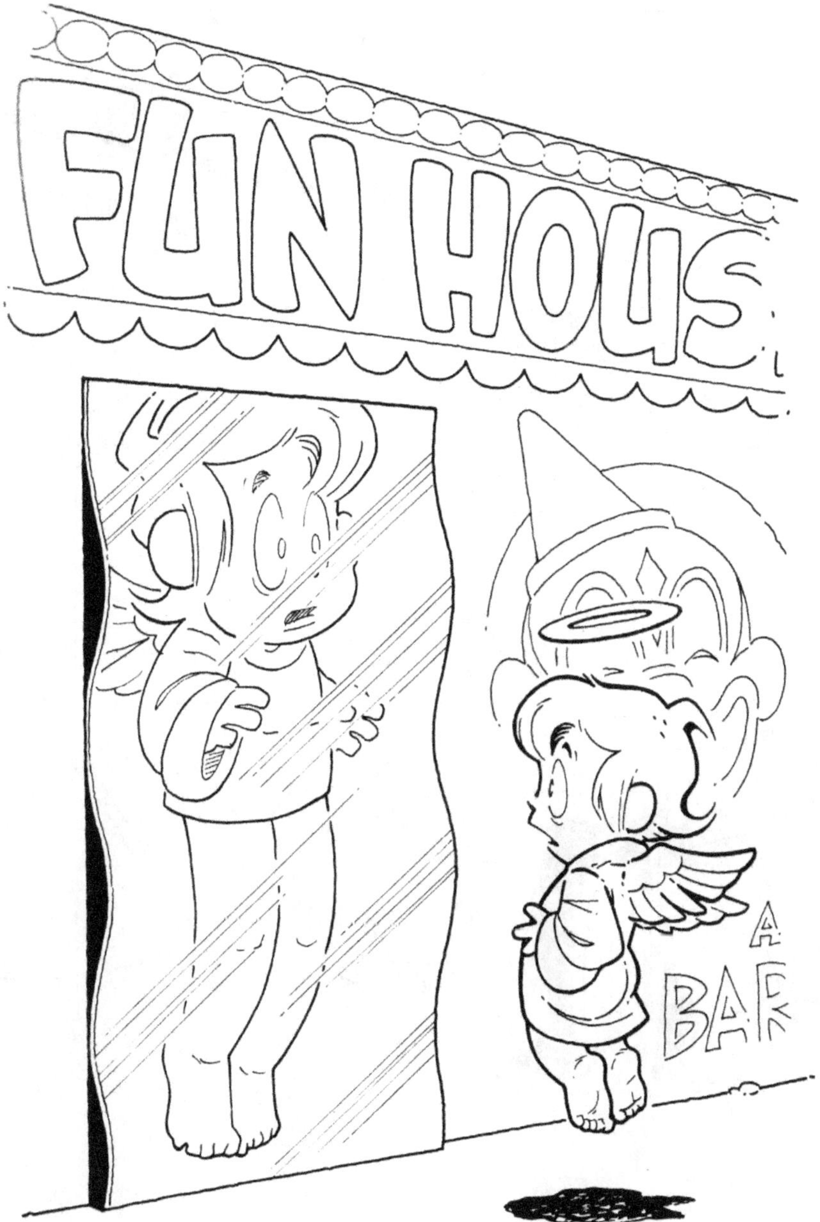
FUN HOUS
A
BAR

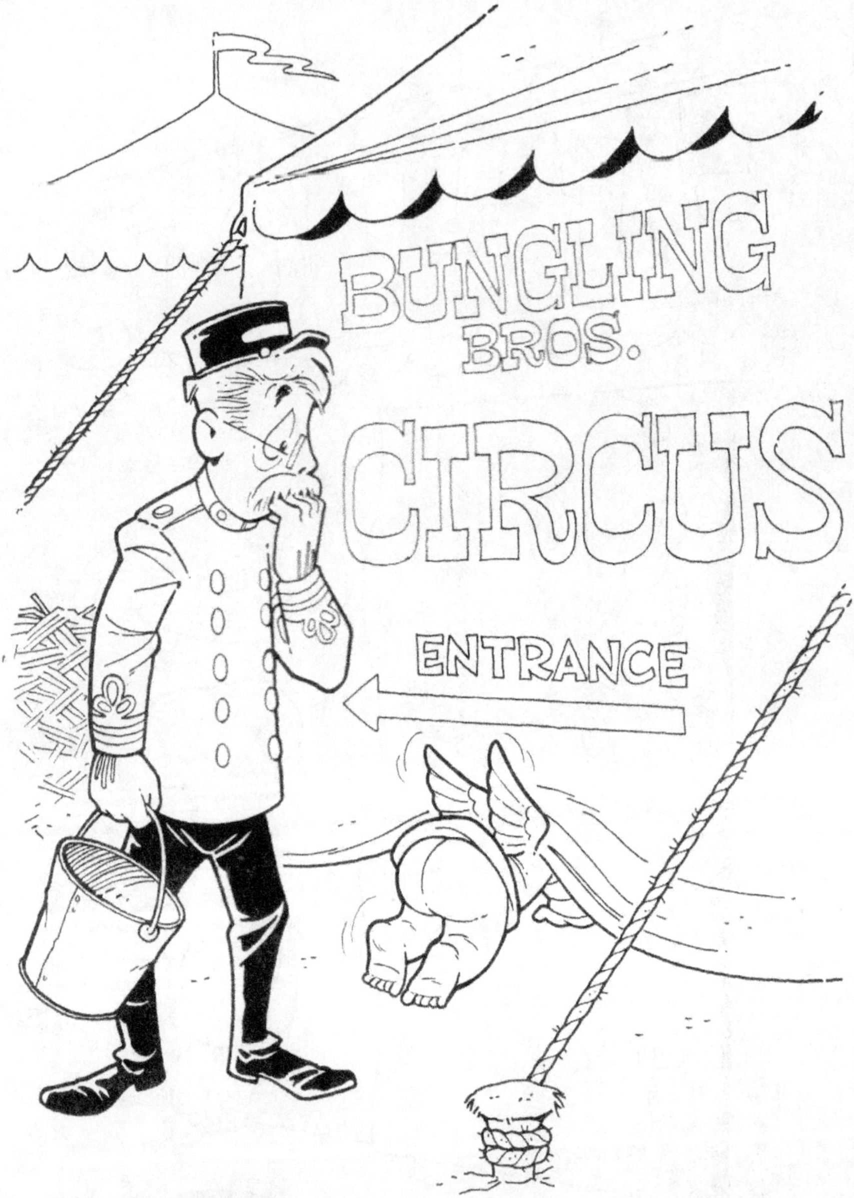
BUNGLING
BROS.
CIRCUS
ENTRANCE

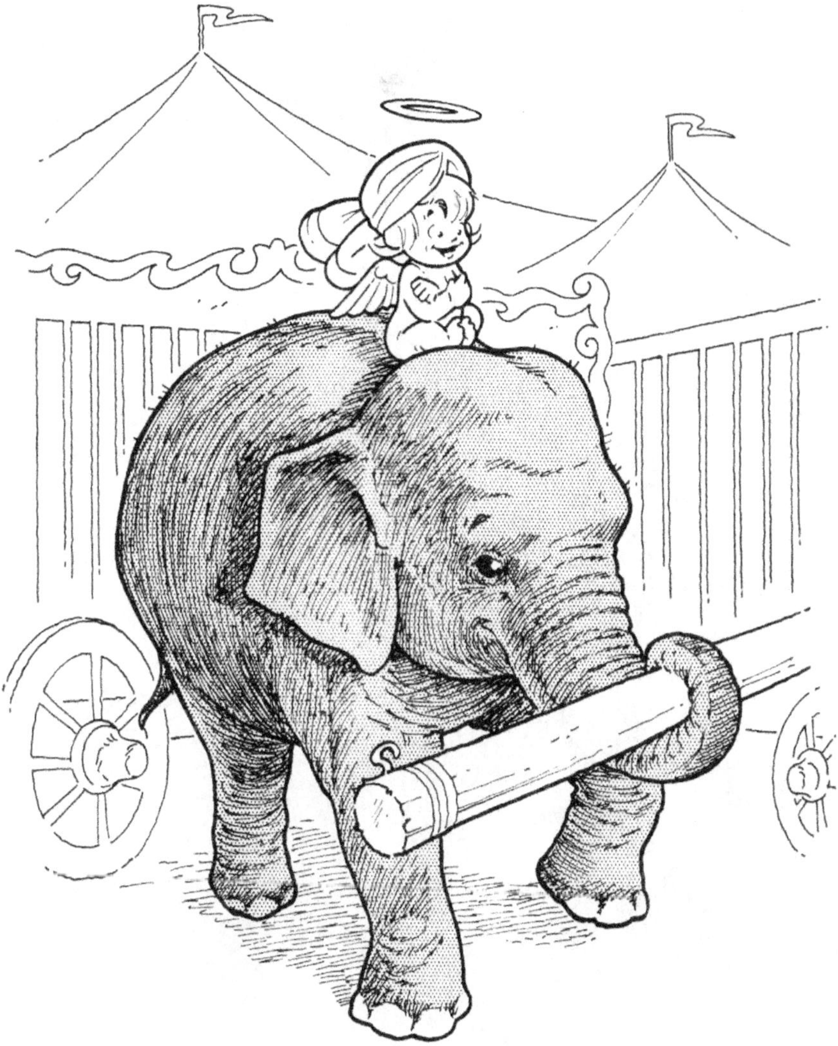

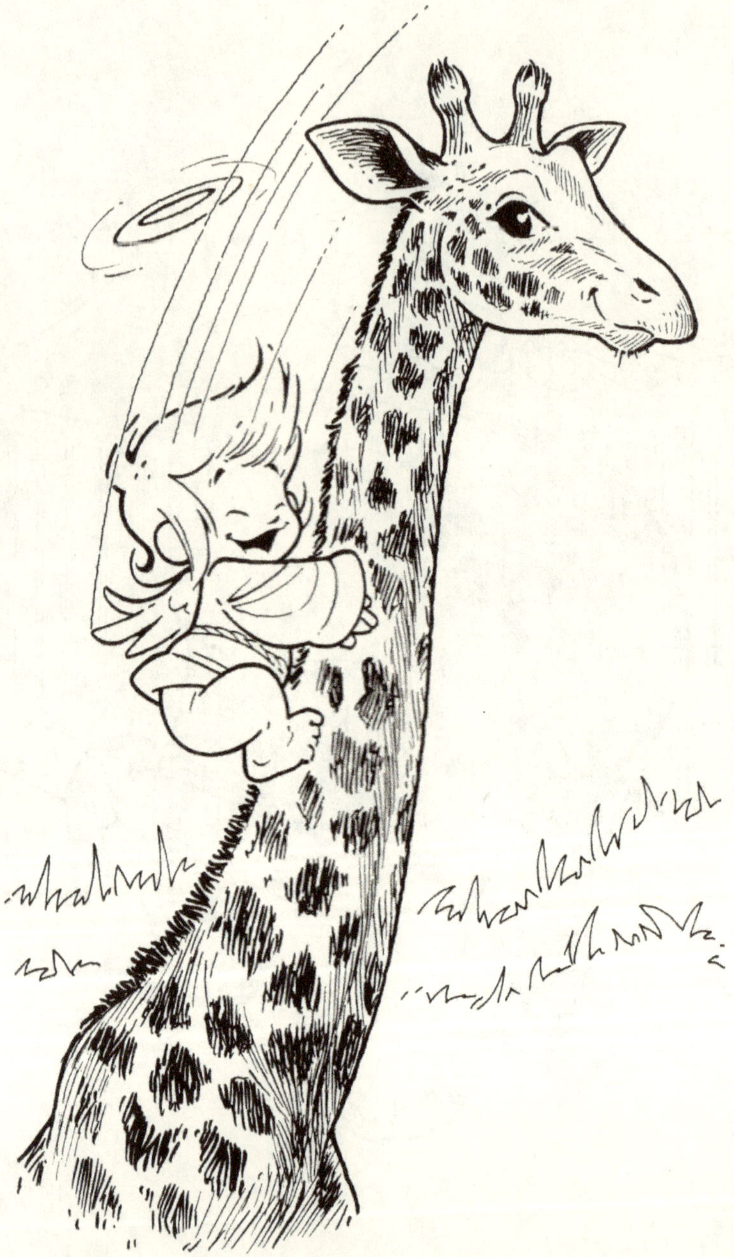

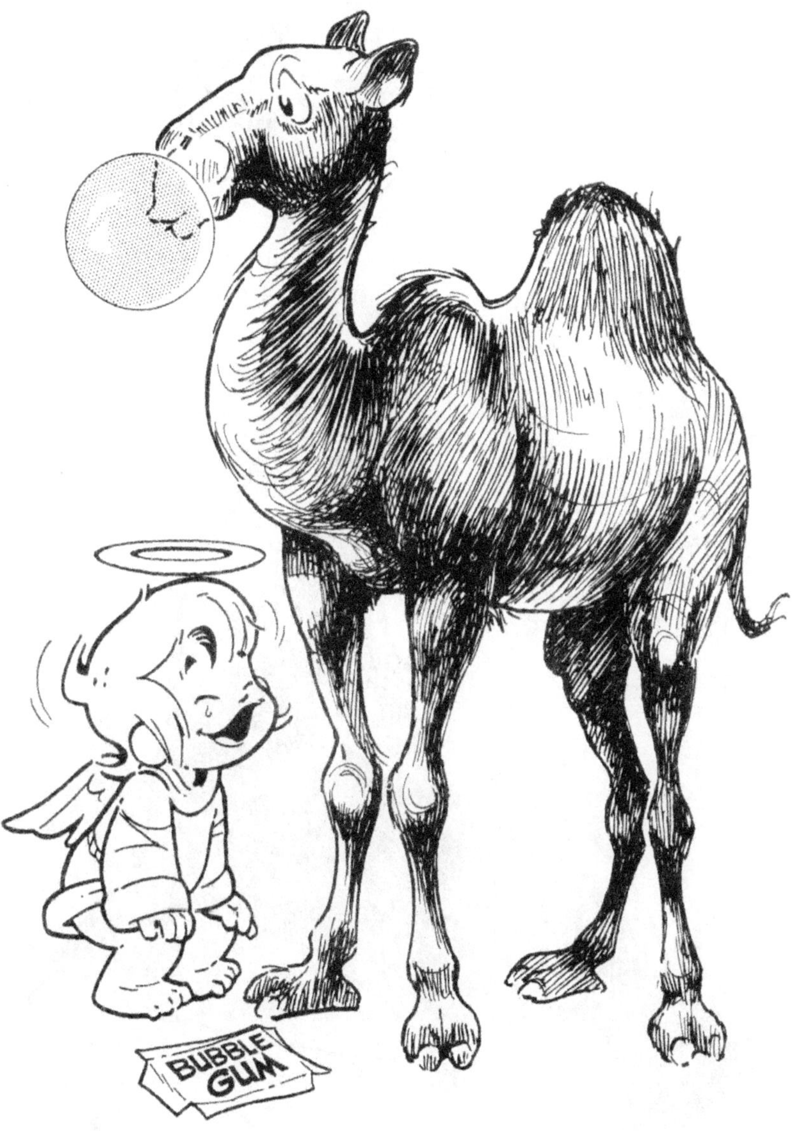
BUBBLE
GUM

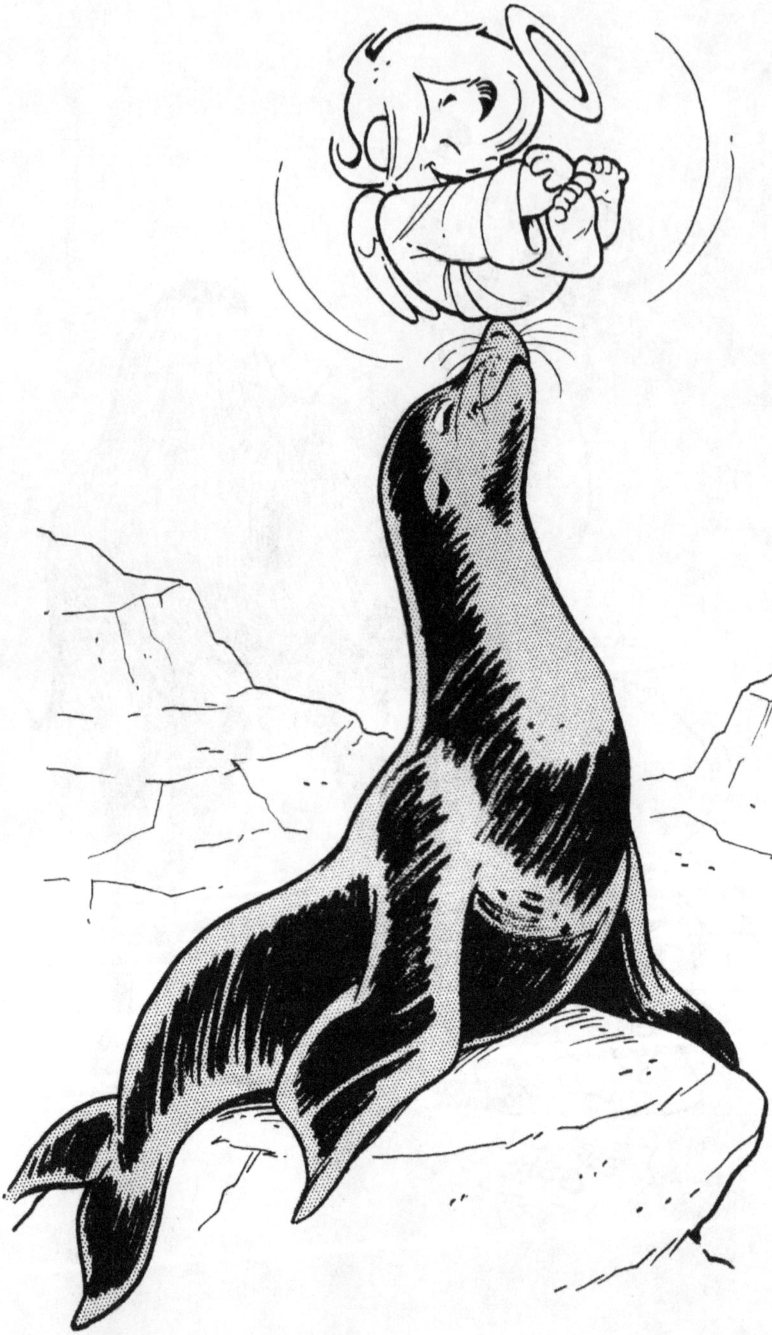

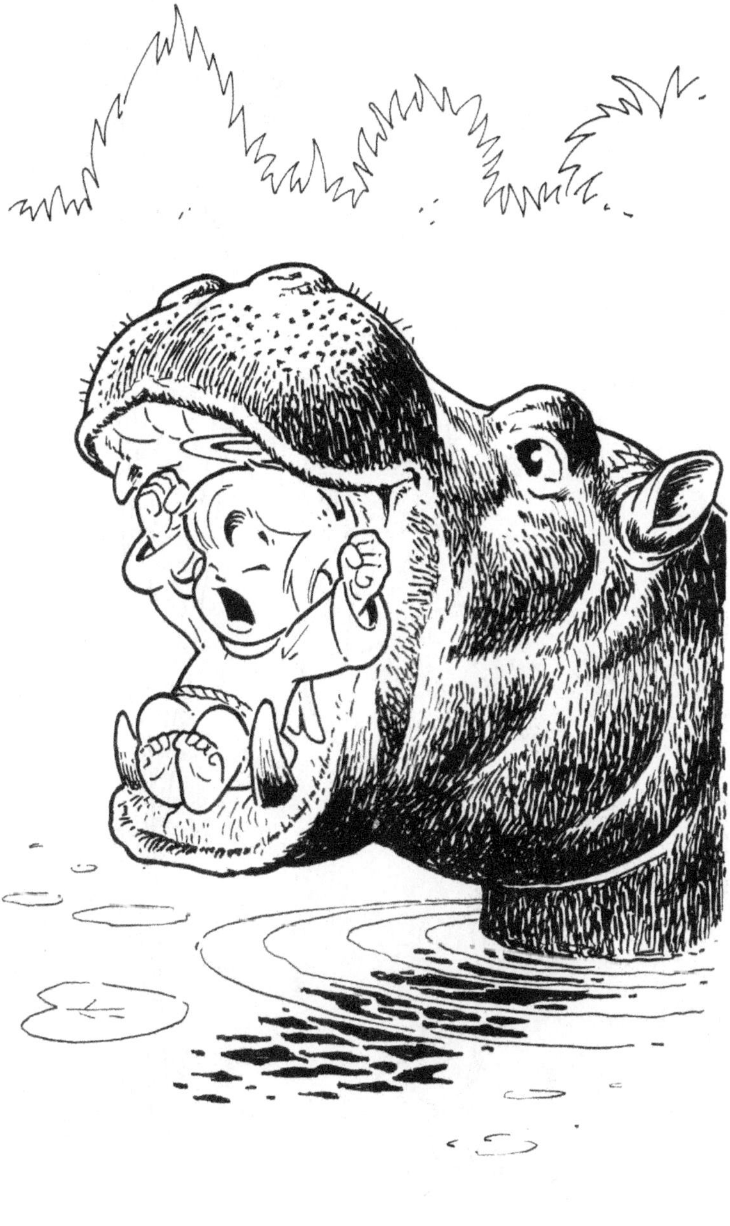

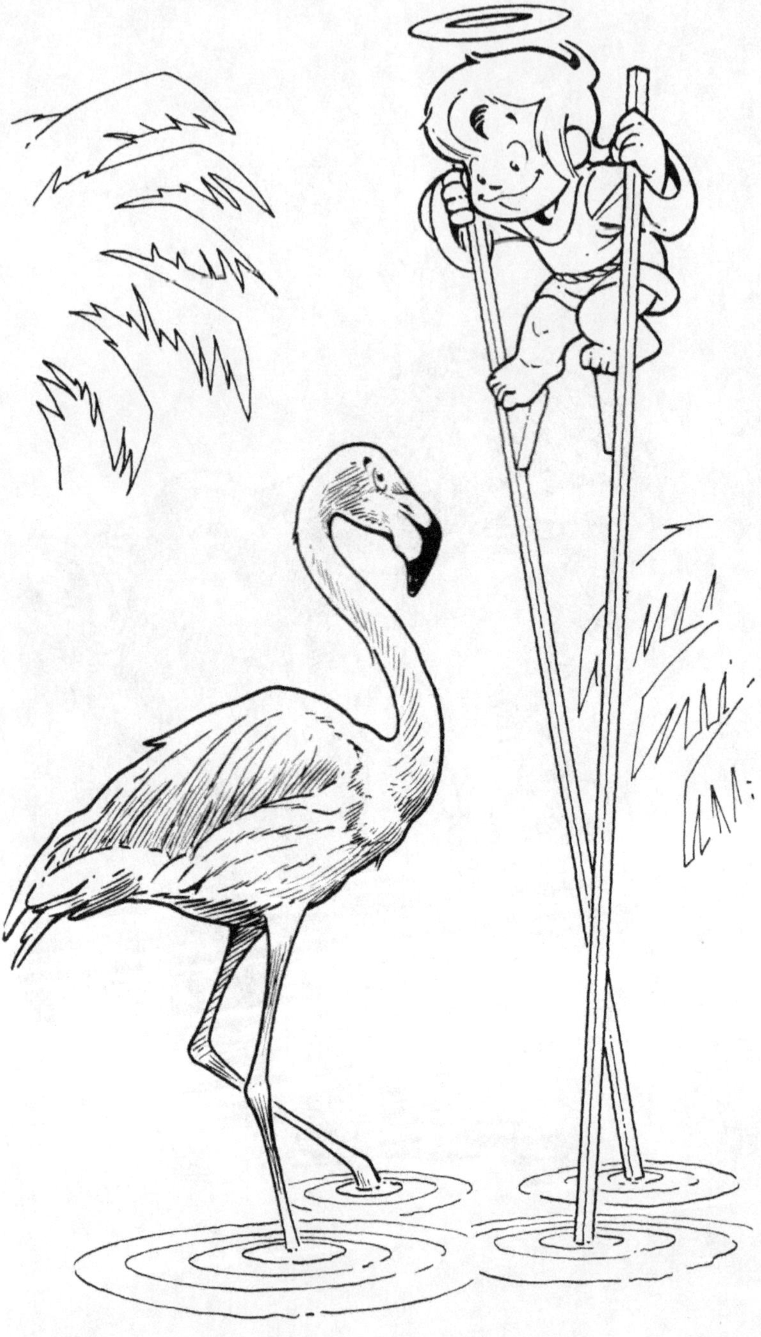

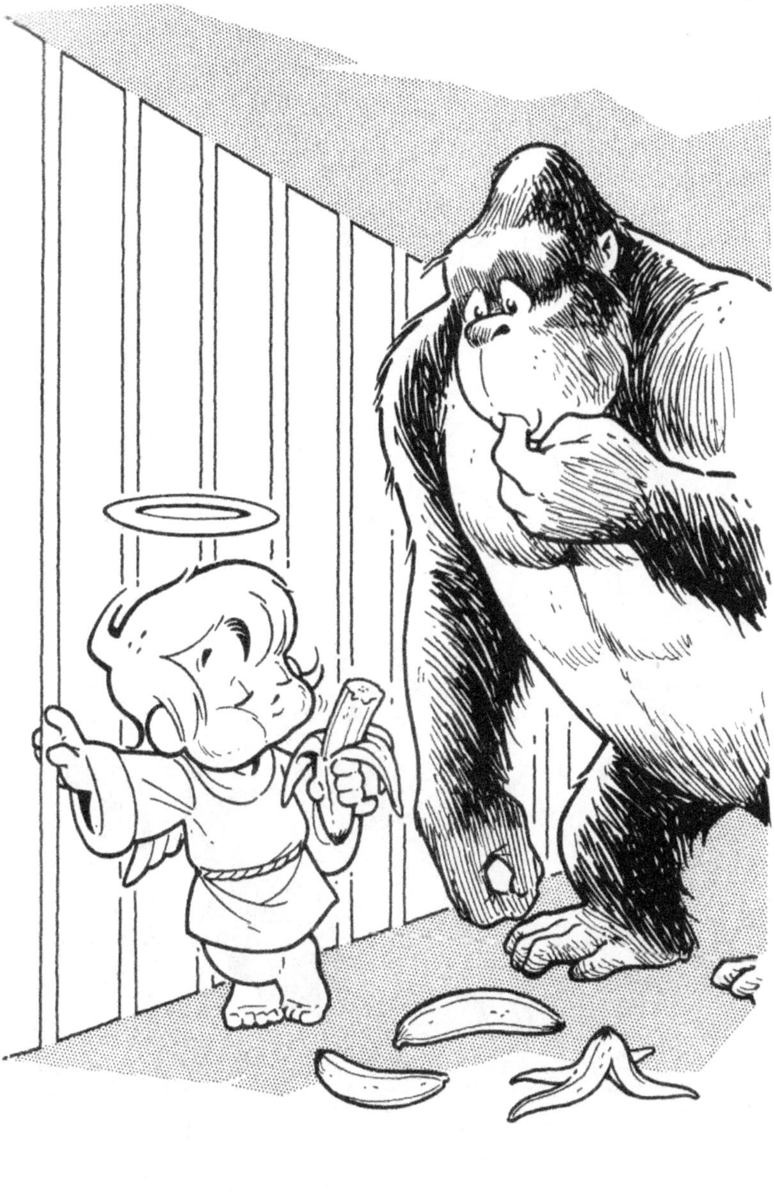

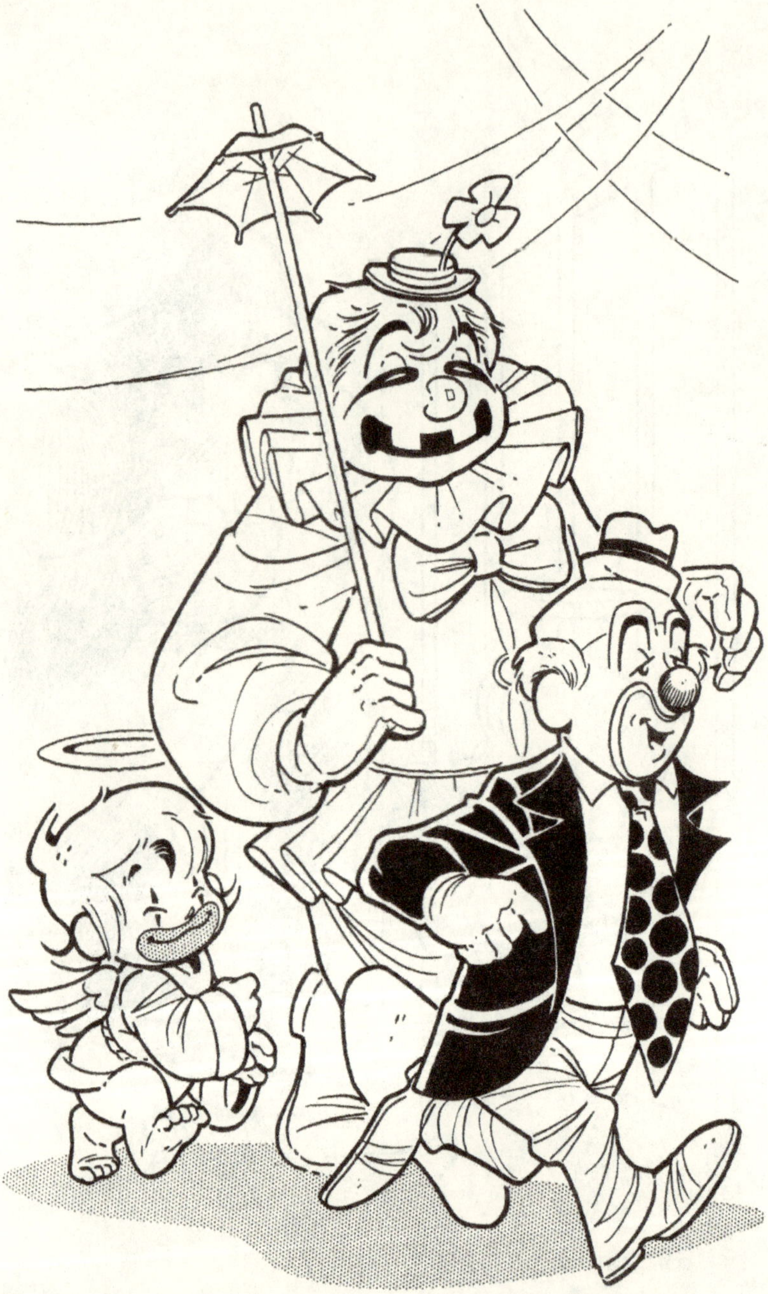

CLIK!

SNAP!

COOKIES

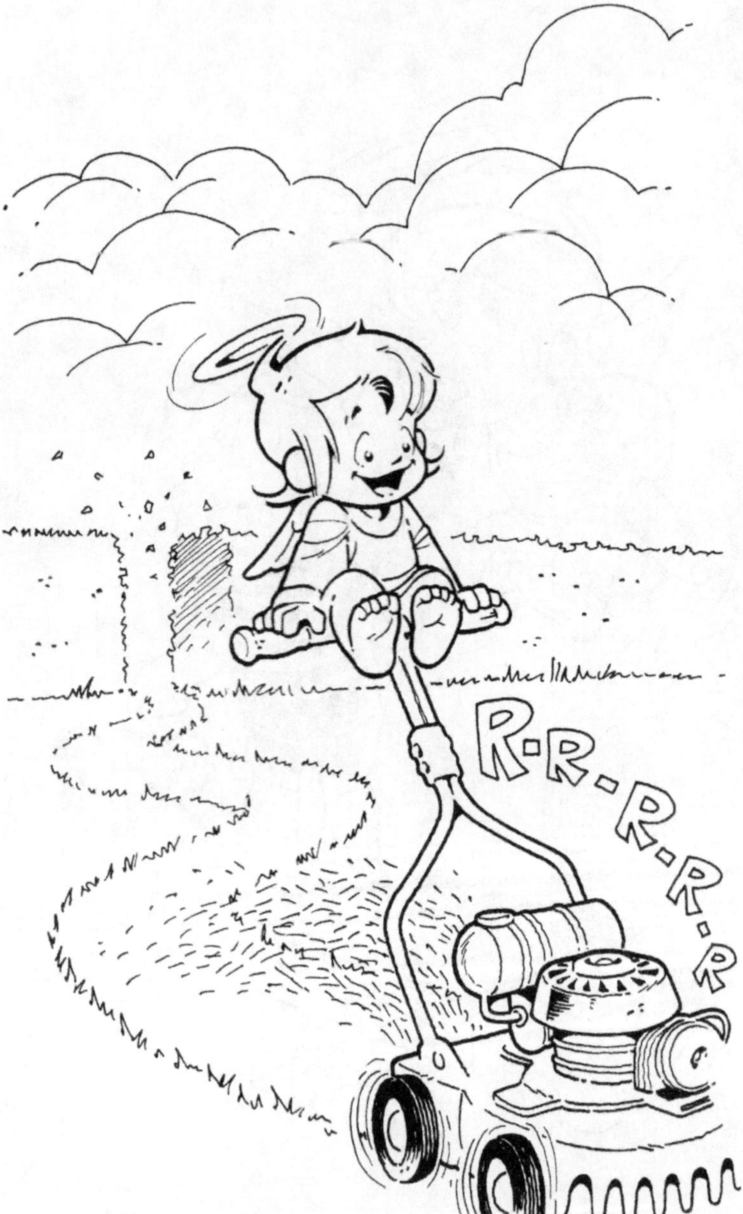
R-R-R-R-R-R-R

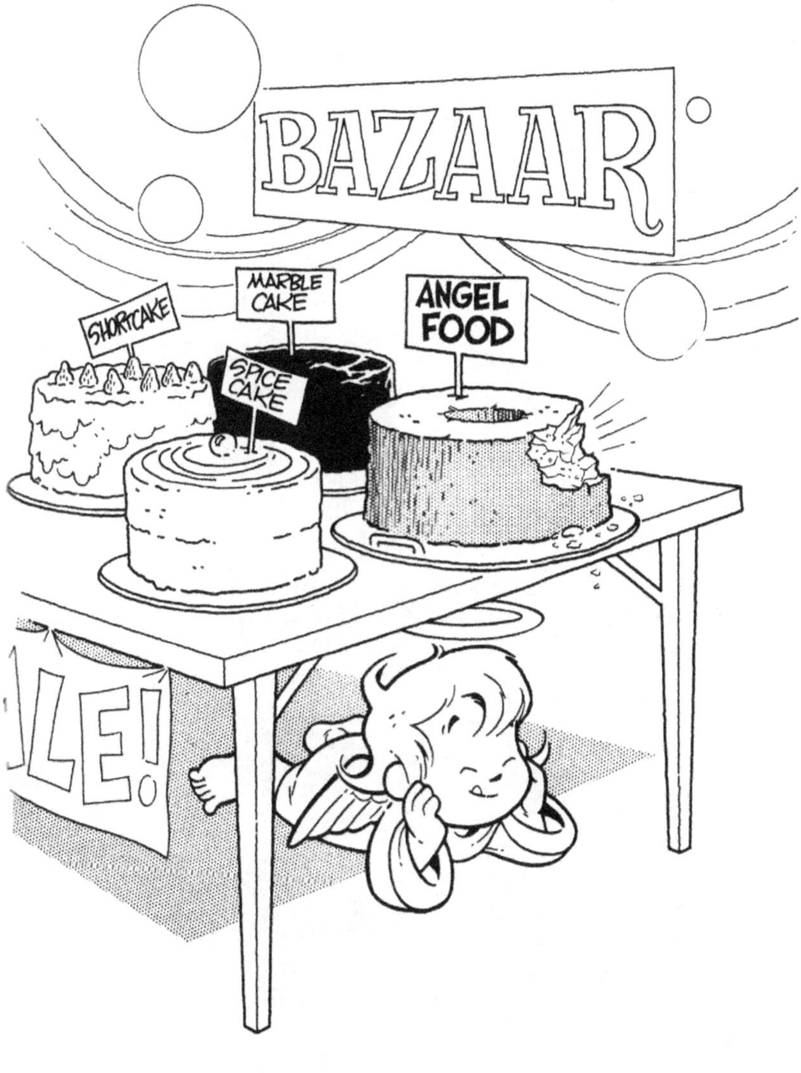
BAZAAR
MARBLE CAKE
SHORTCAKE
ANGEL FOOD
SPICE CAKE
LE!

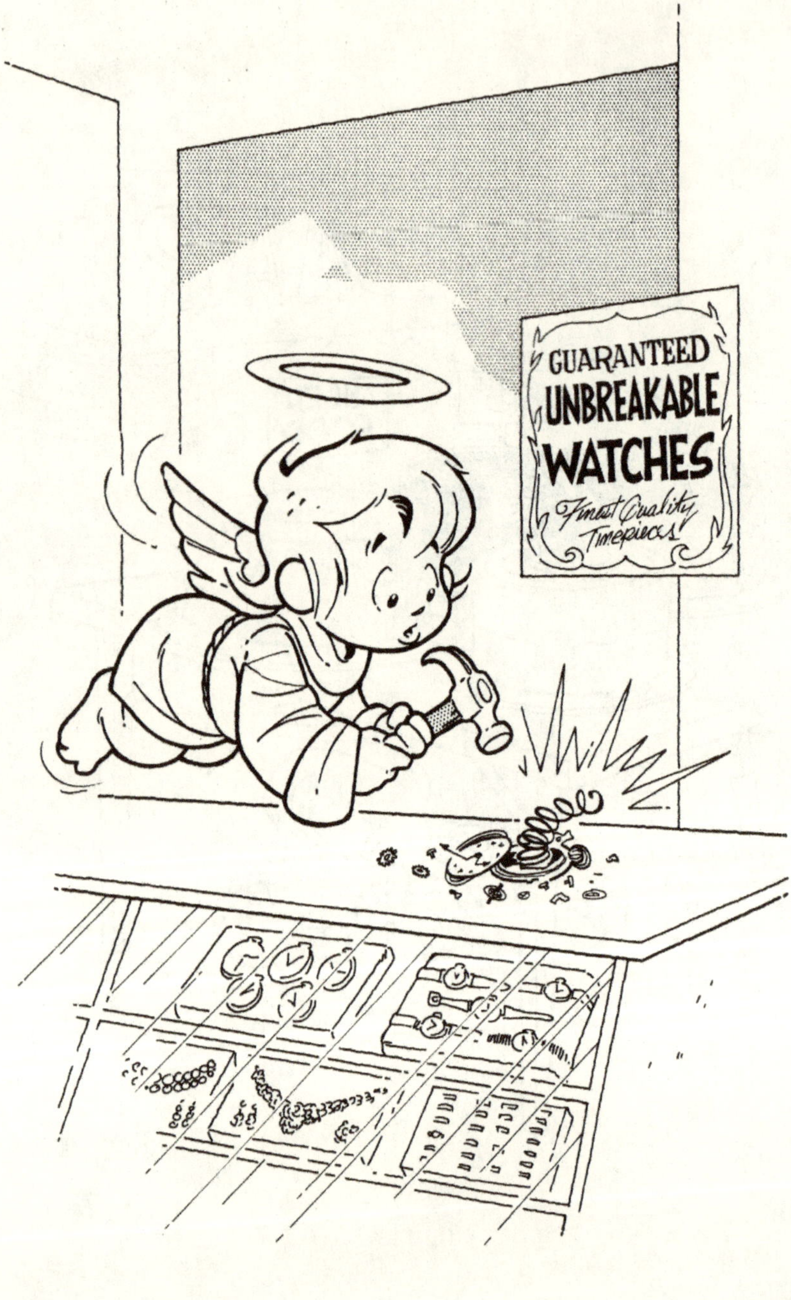
GUARANTEED
UNBREAKABLE
WATCHES
Finest Quality
Timepieces!

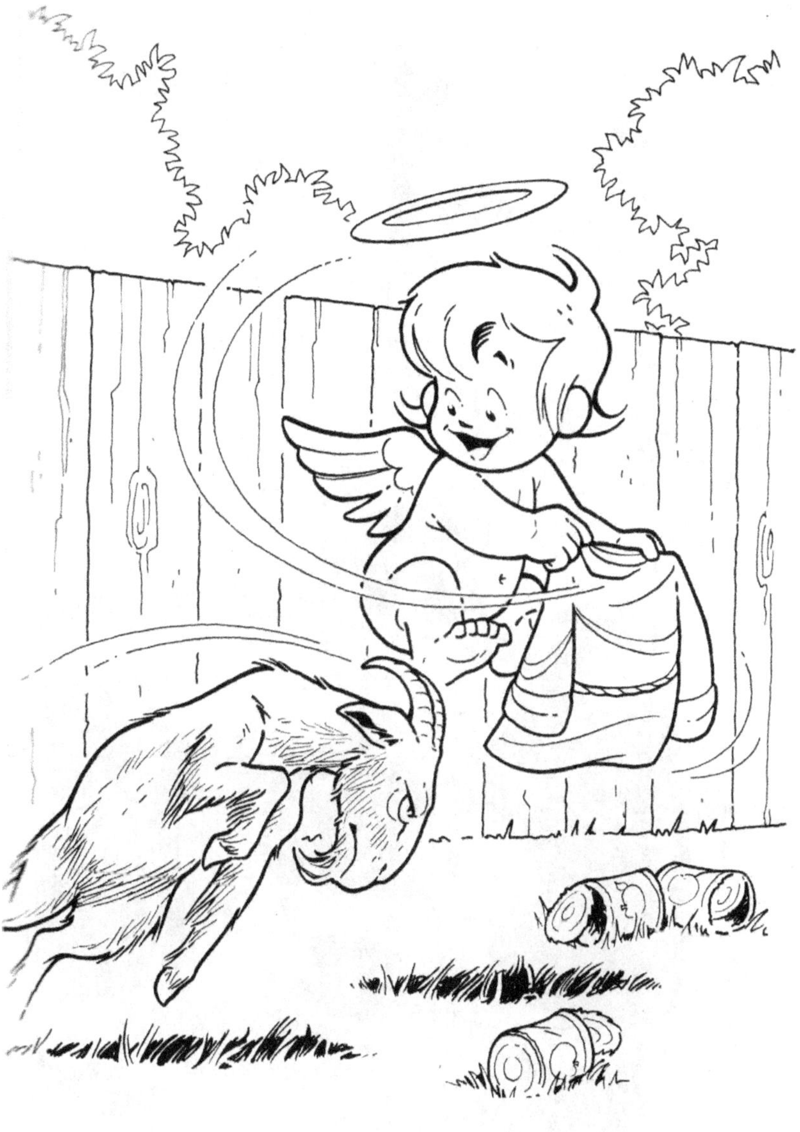

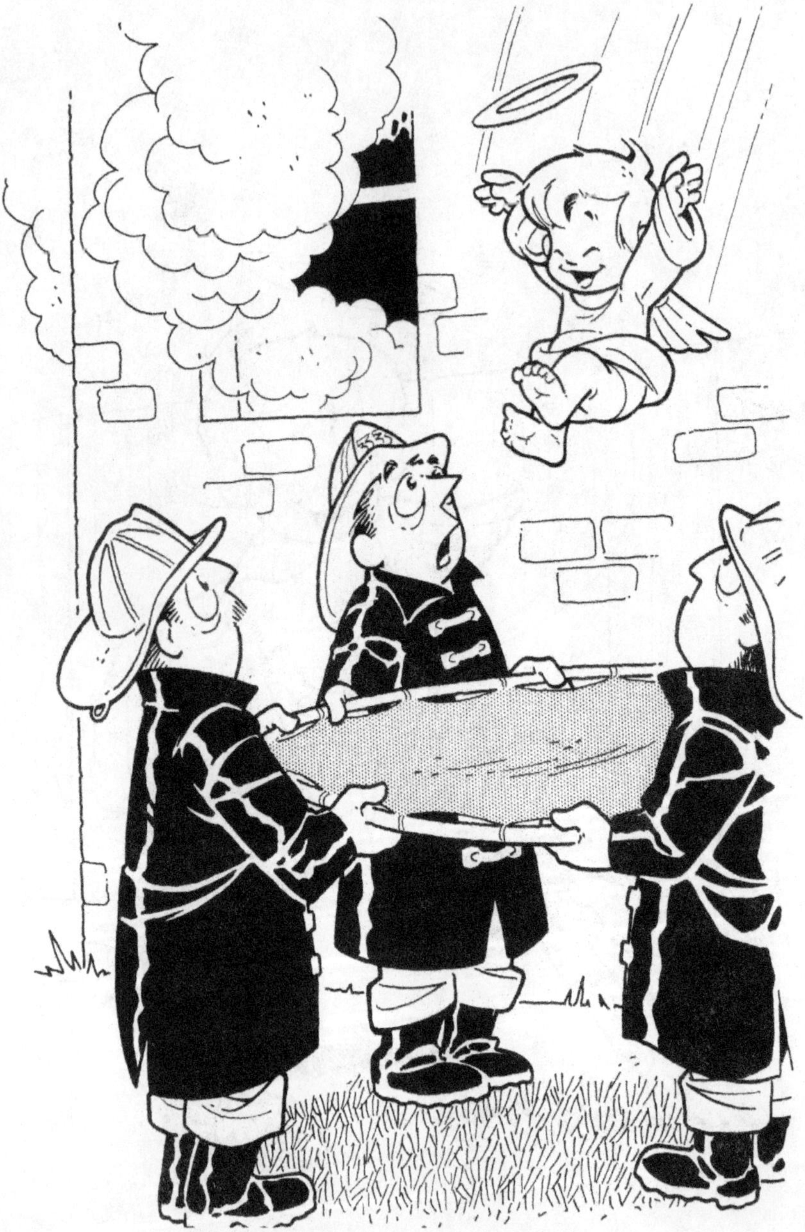

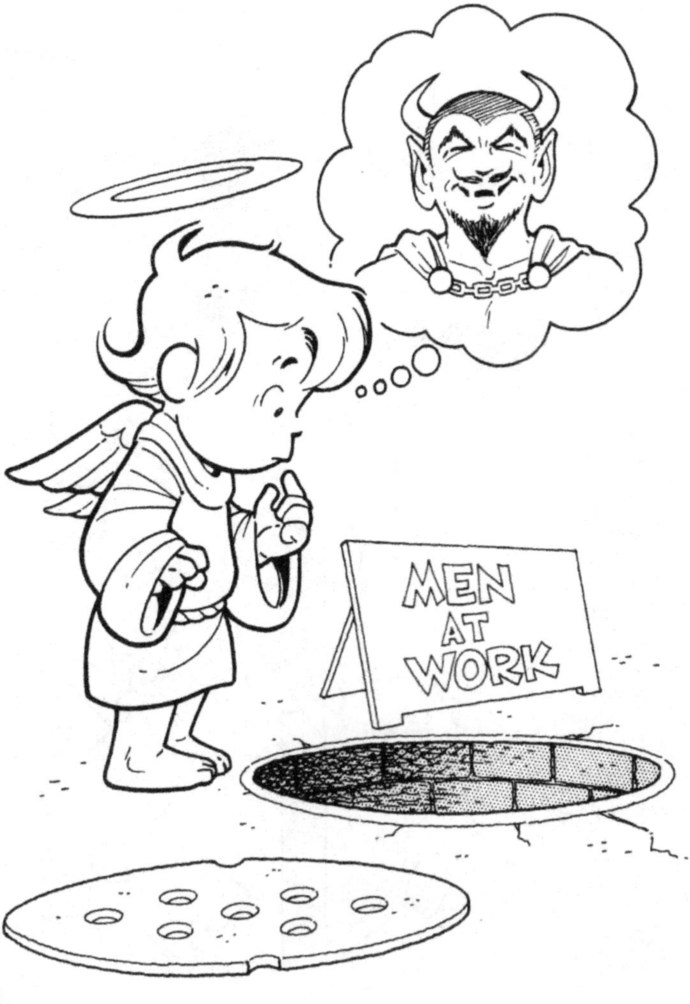

MEN
AT
WORK

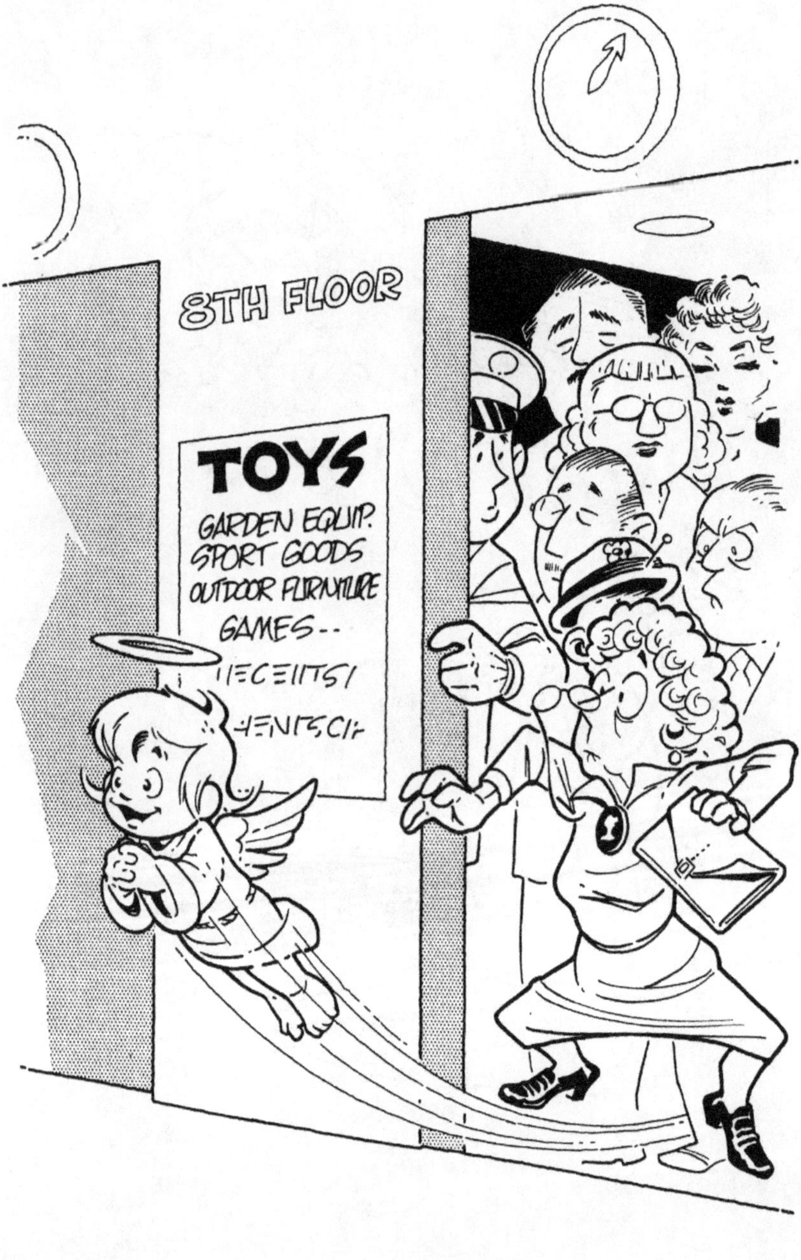
8TH FLOOR
TOYS
GARDEN EQUIP.
SPORT GOODS
OUTDOOR FURNITURE
GAMES--

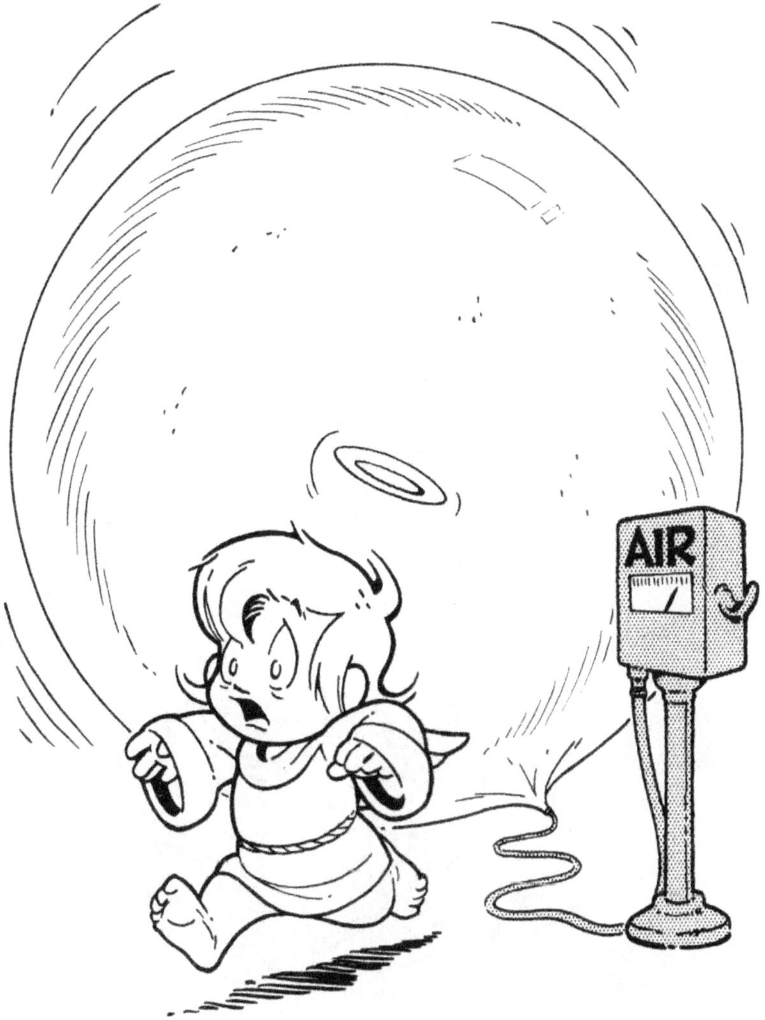
AIR

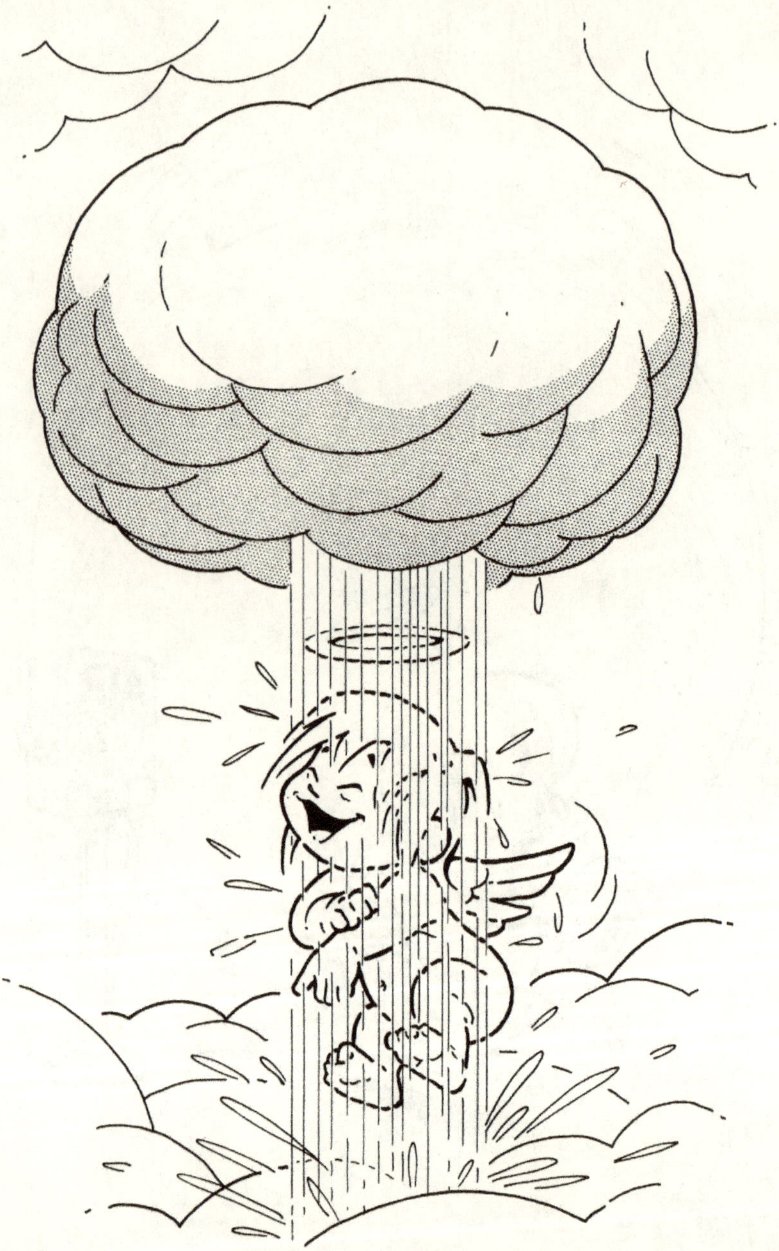

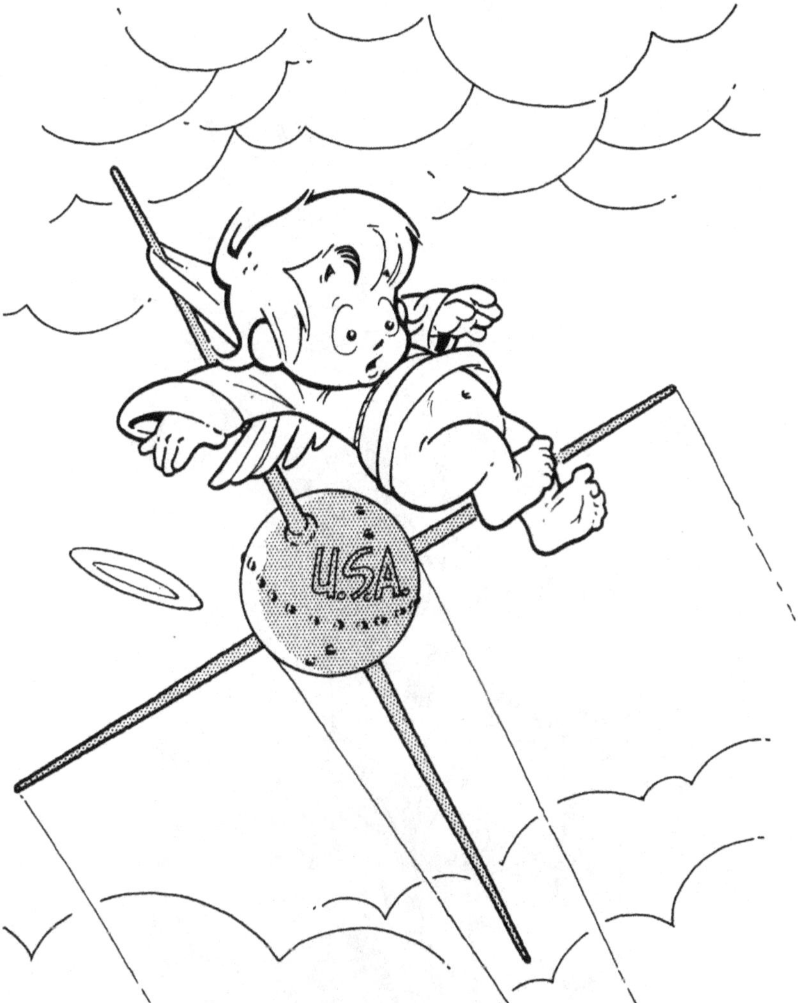
U.S.A.

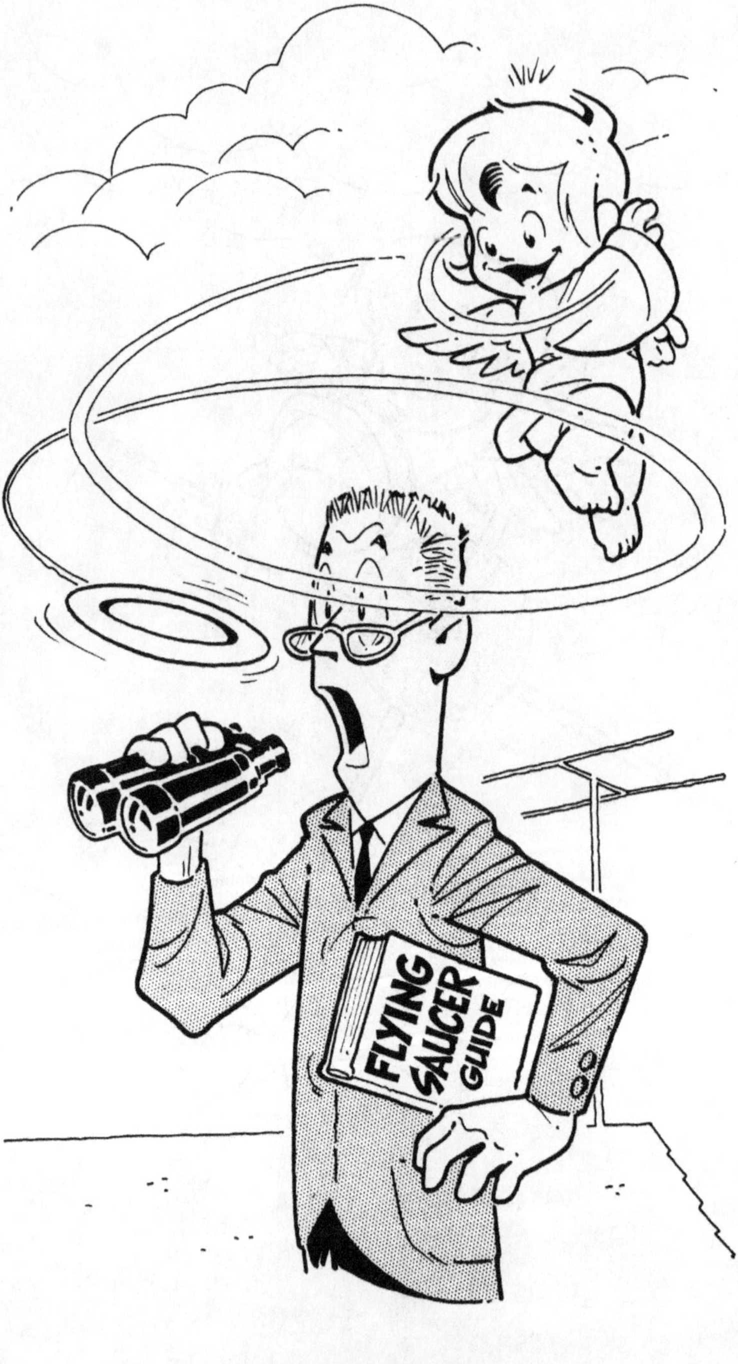
FLYING SAUCER GUIDE

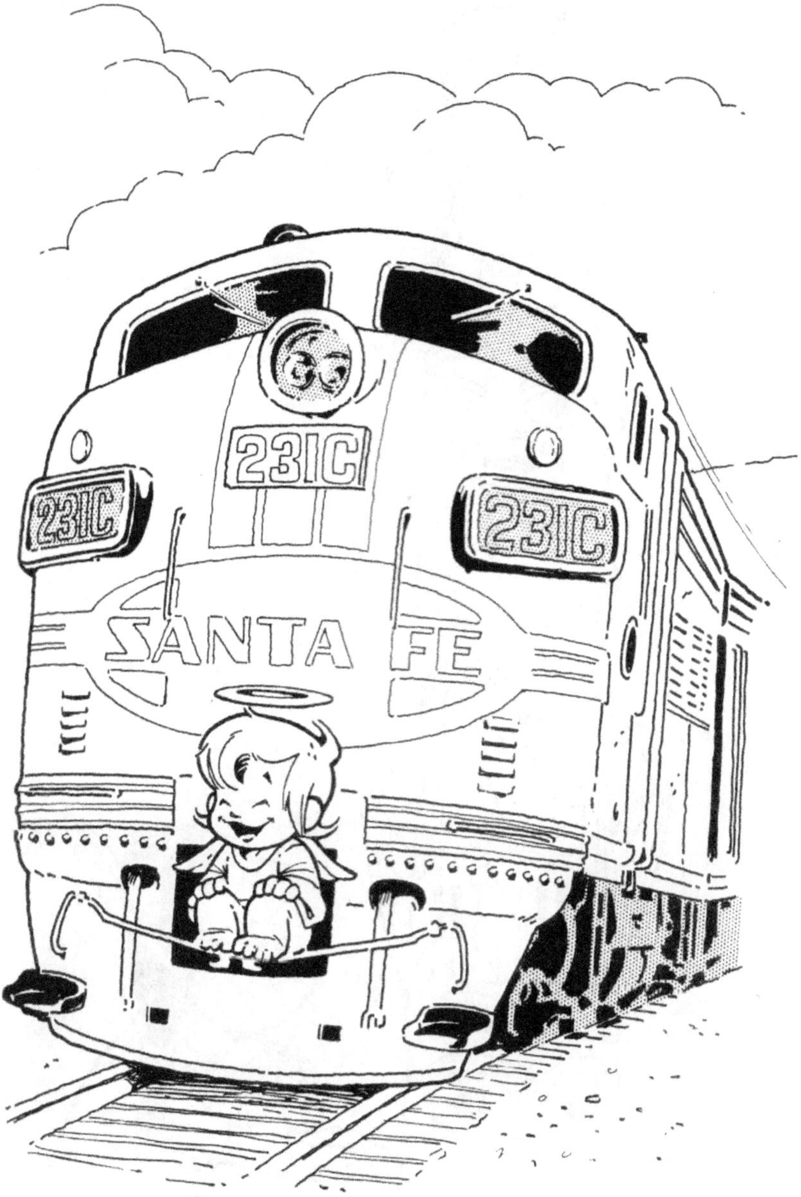
231C
231C
231C
SANTA FE

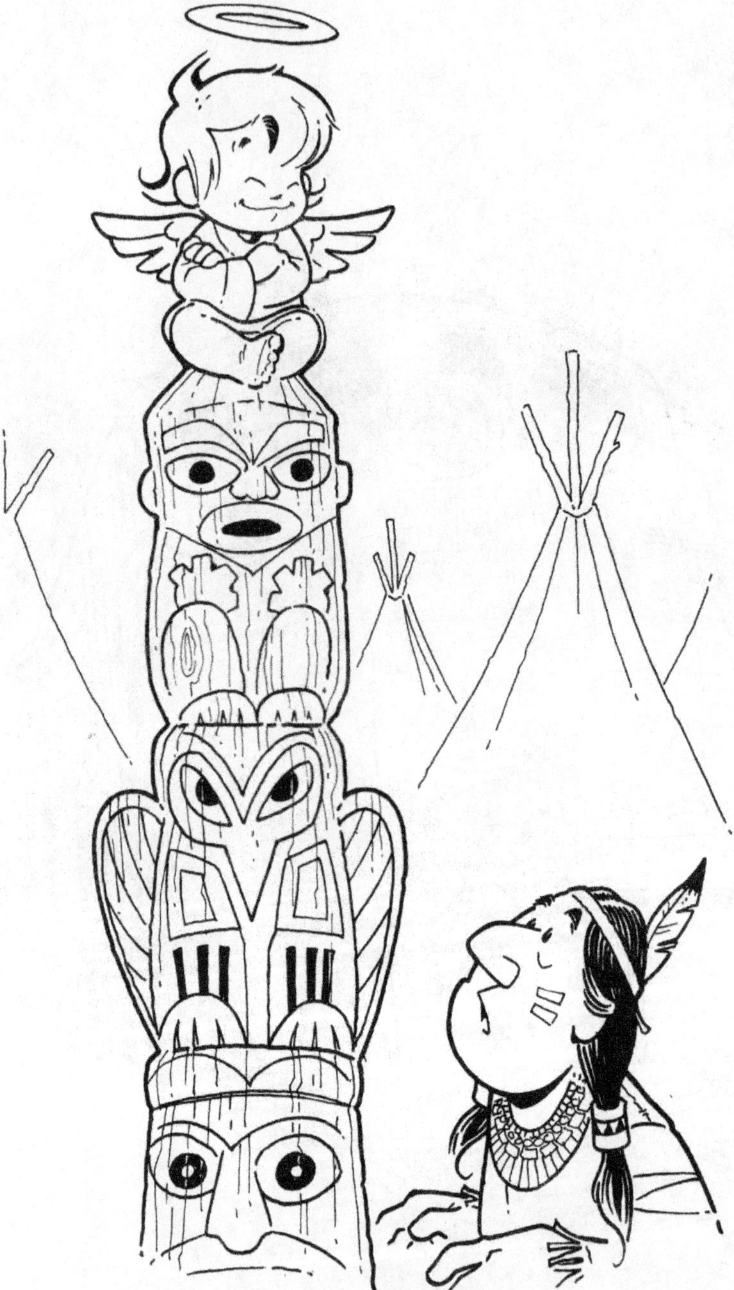

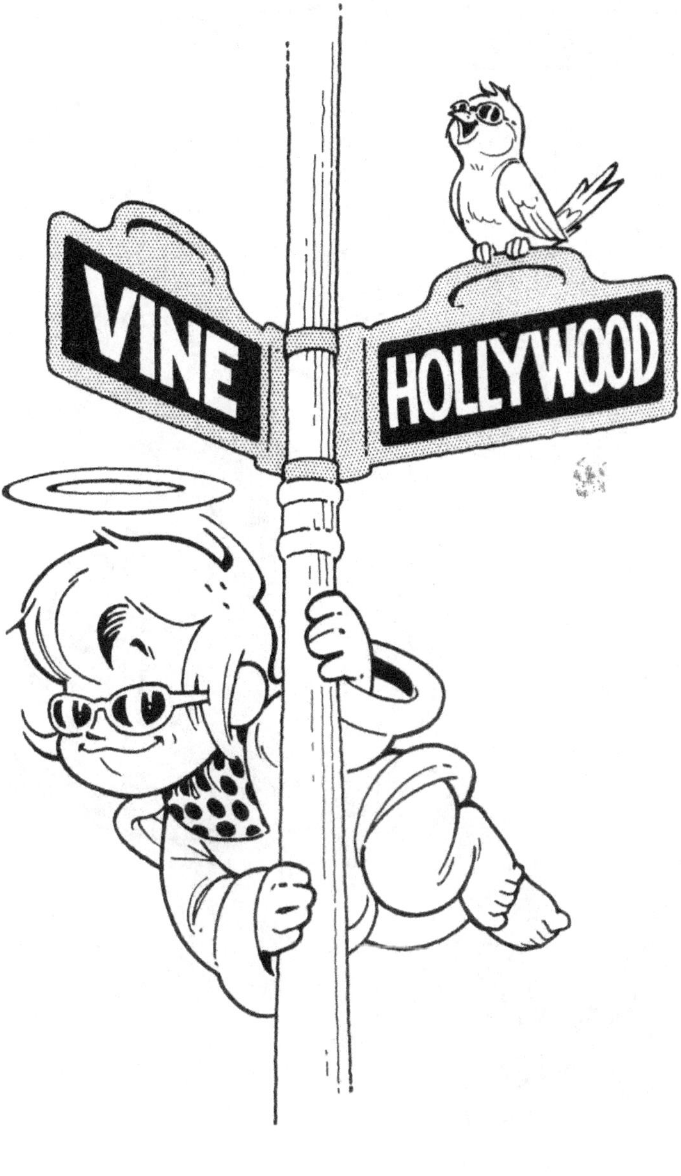
VINE
HOLLYWOOD

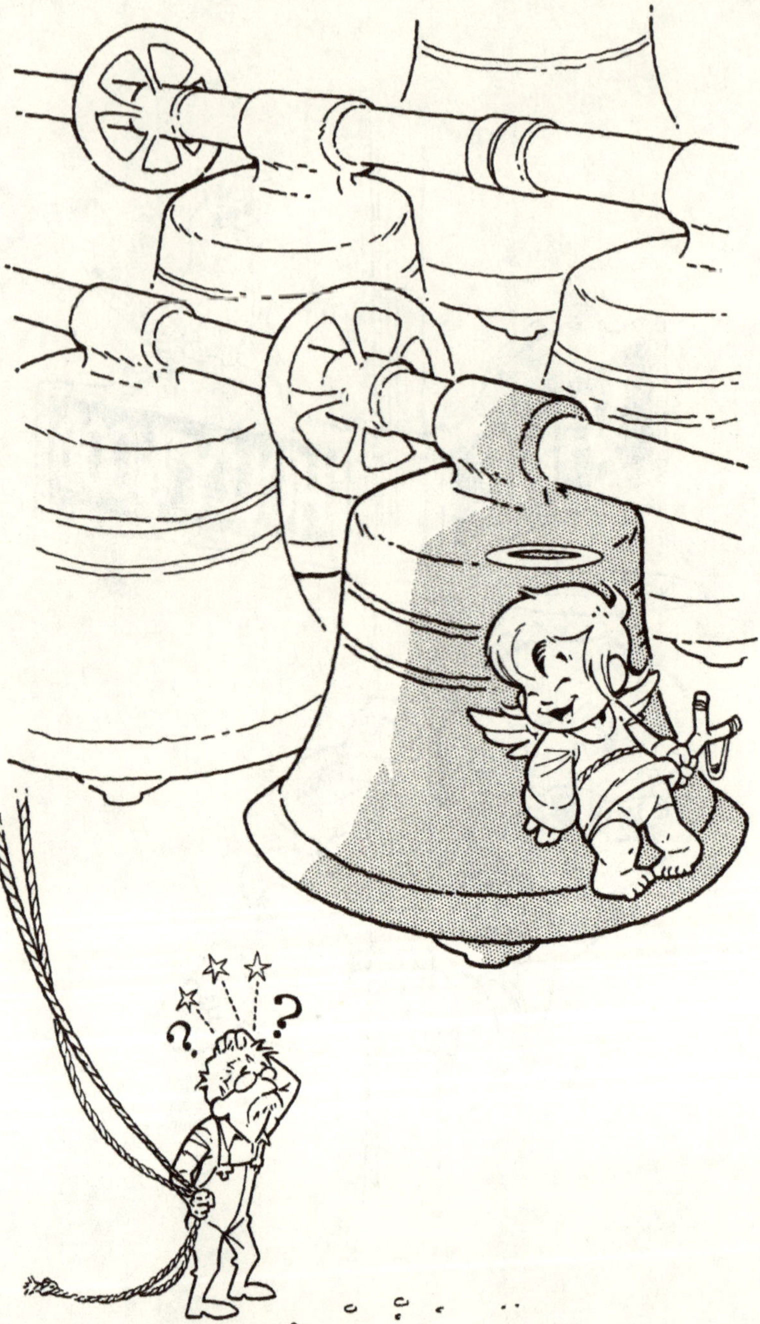

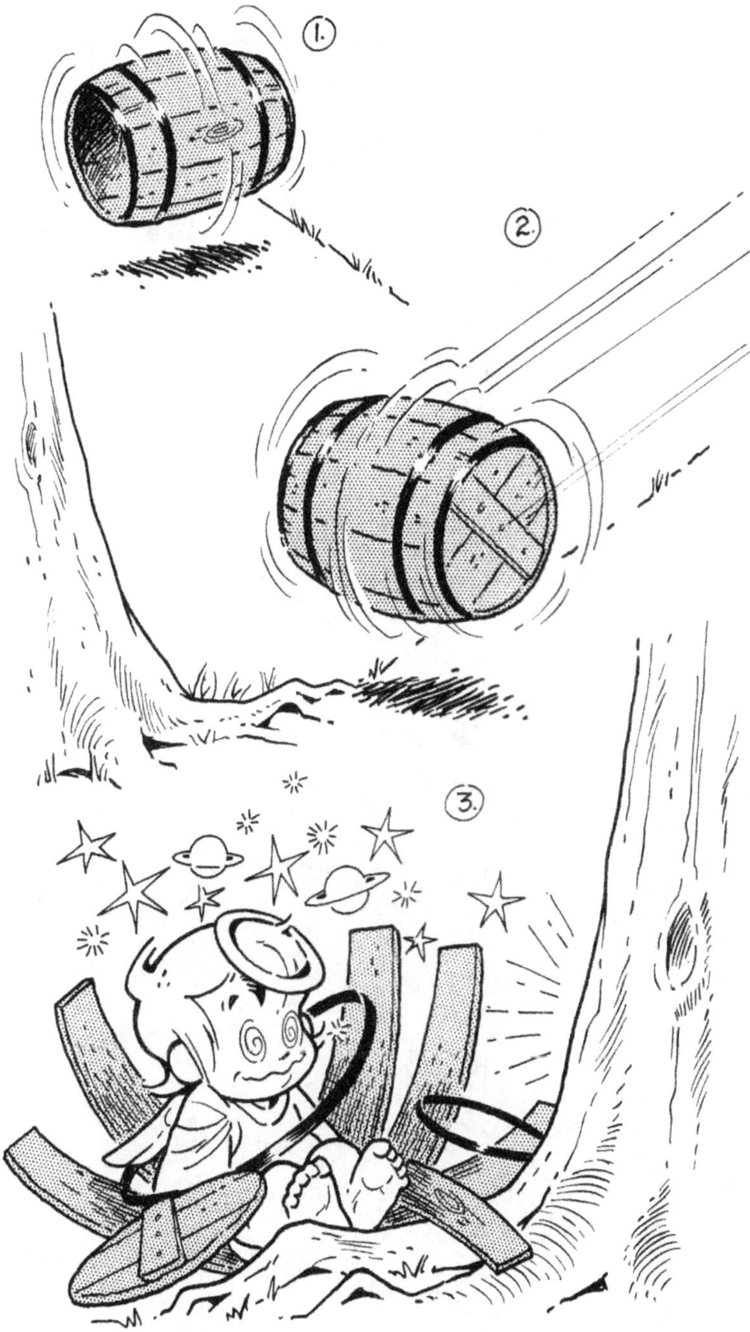
1.
2.
3.

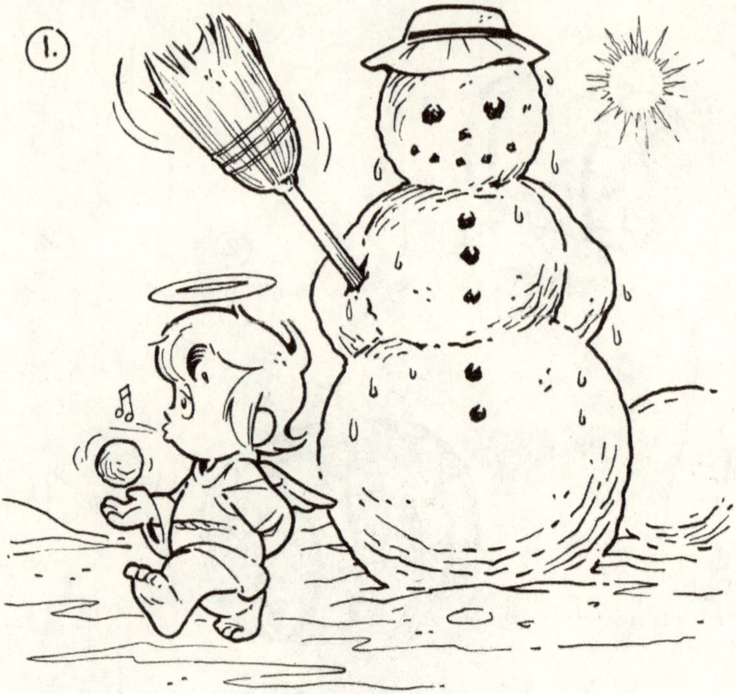
1.

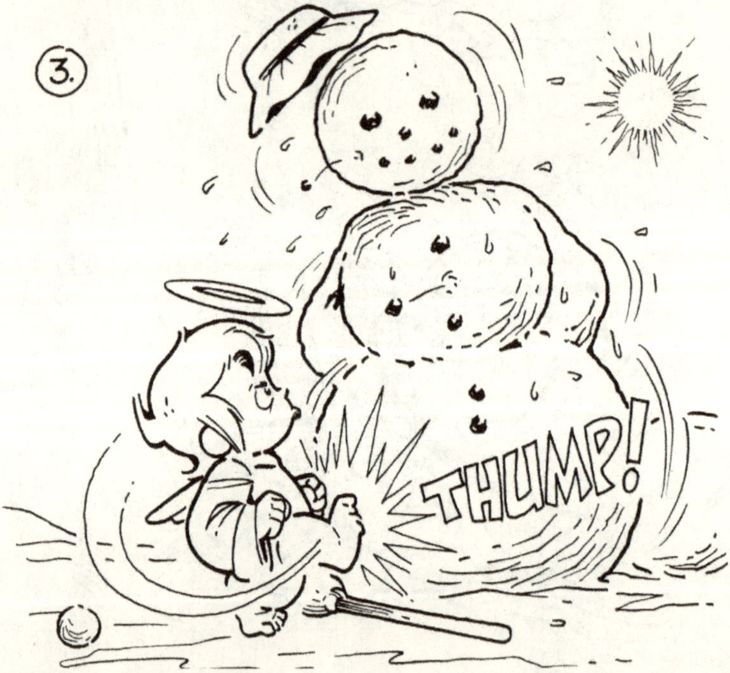
3.
THUMP!

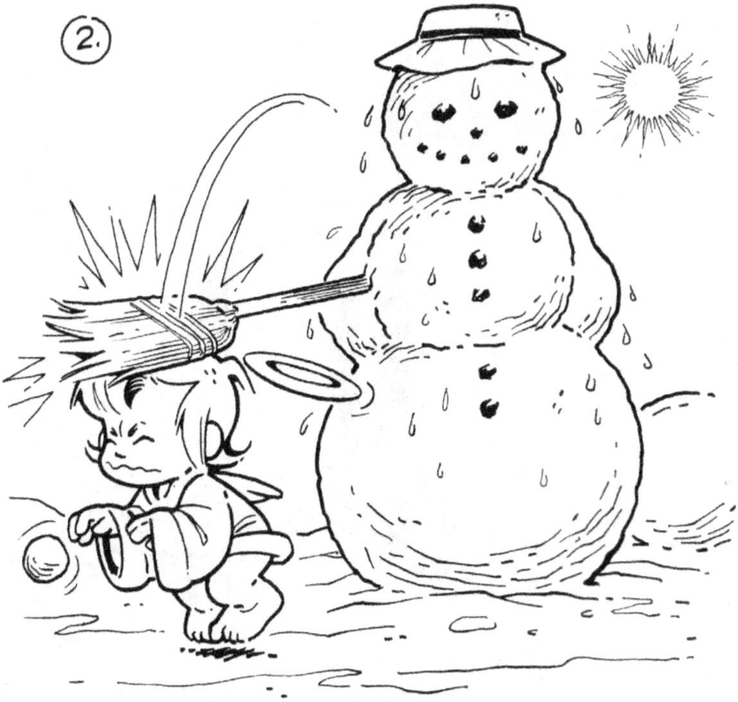
2.

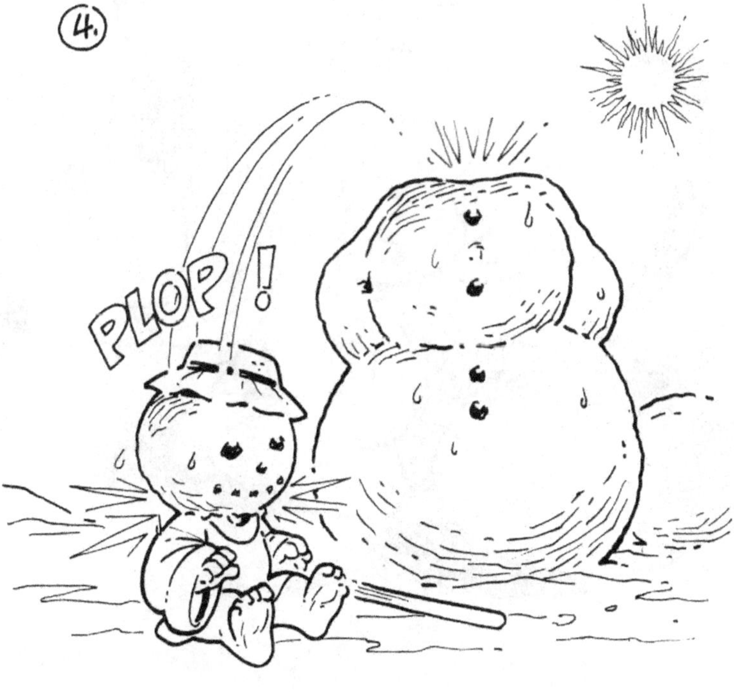
4.
PLOP!

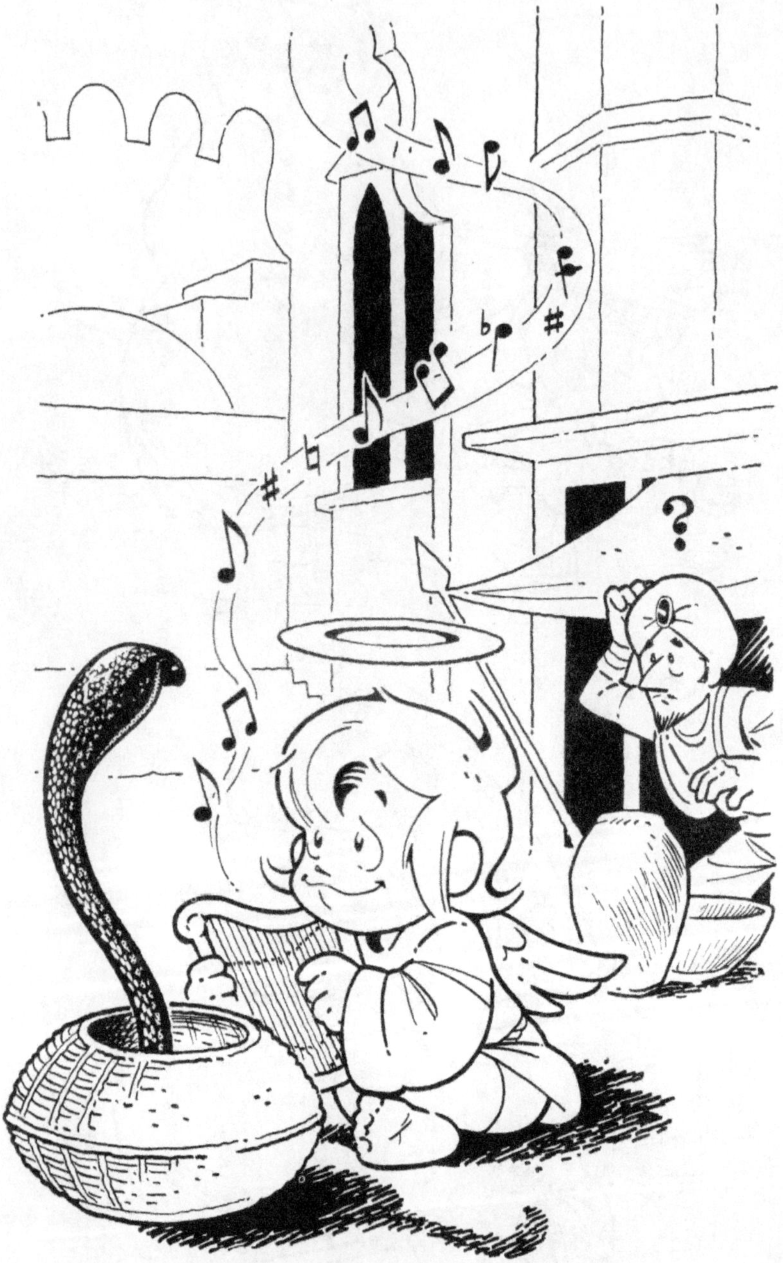
?

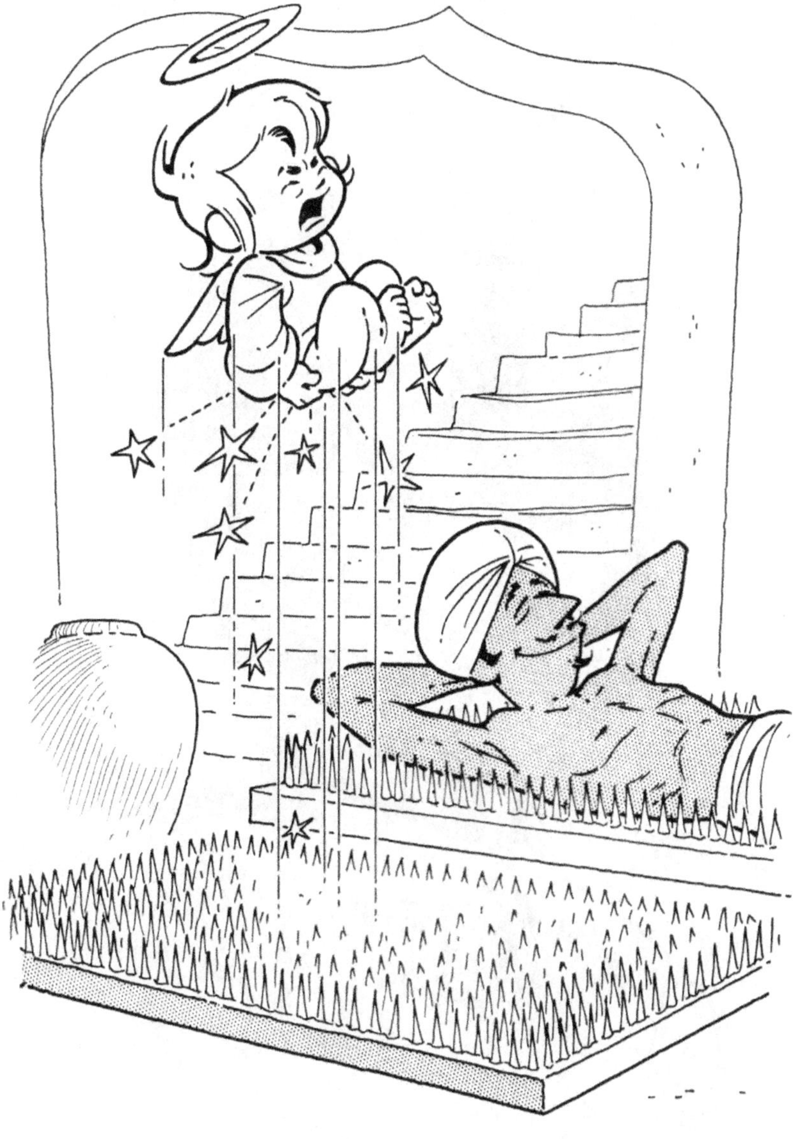

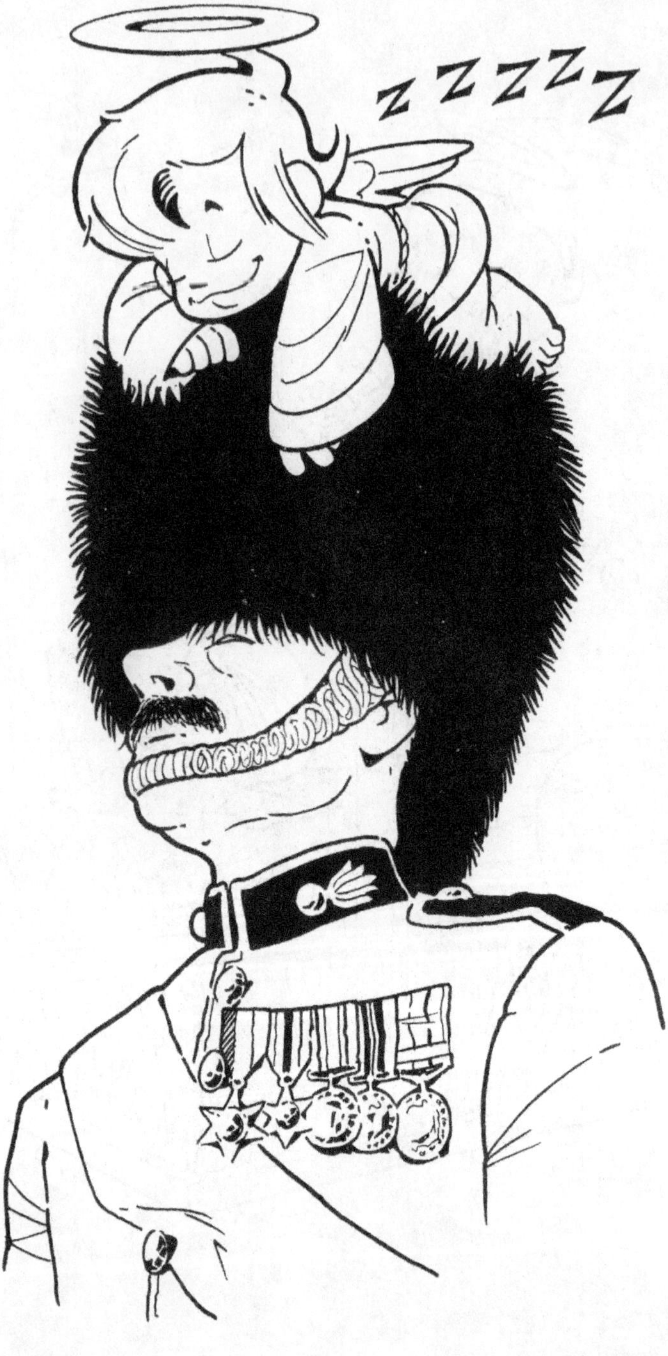
z z z z z z

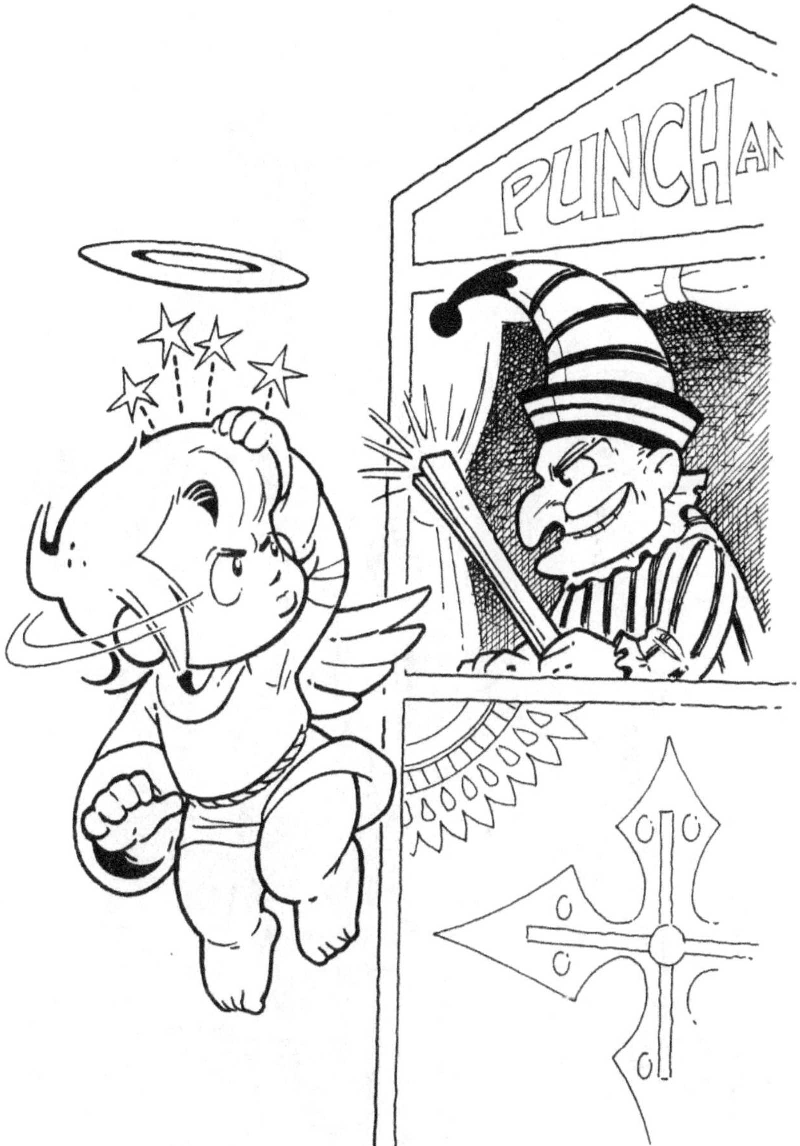
PUNCH

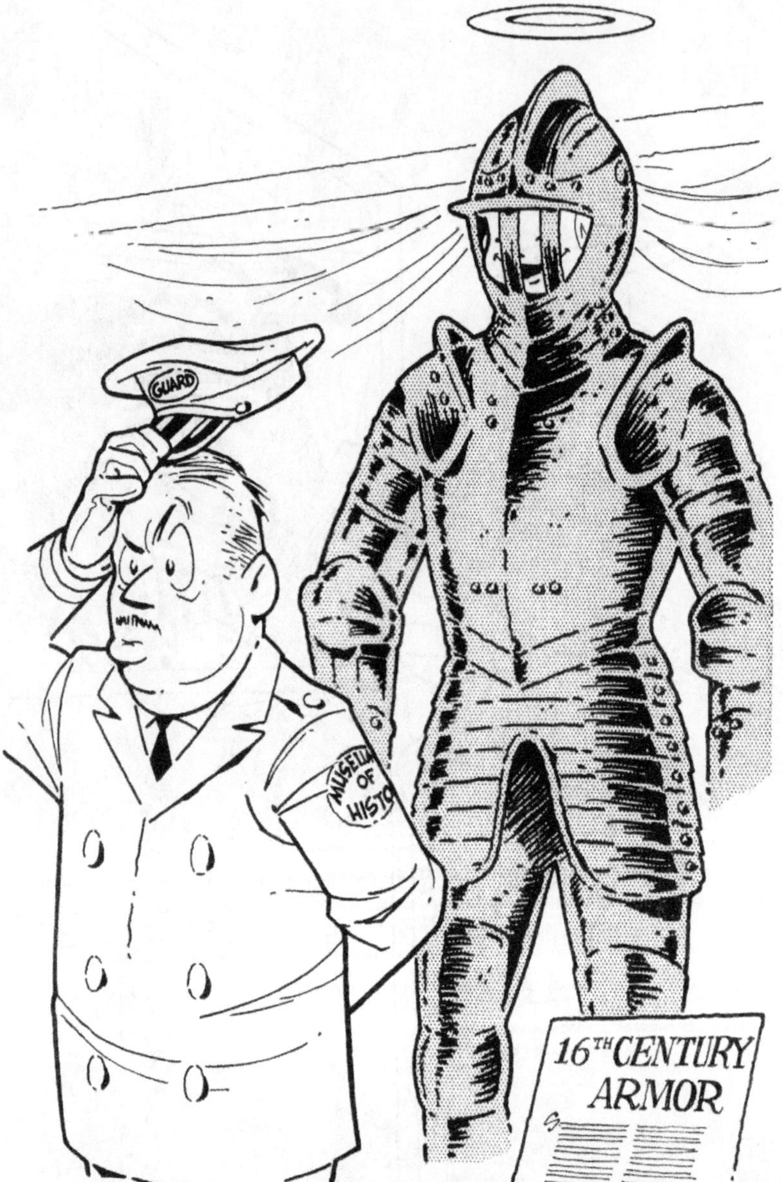
GUARD
MUSEUM OF HISTO
16TH CENTURY ARMOR

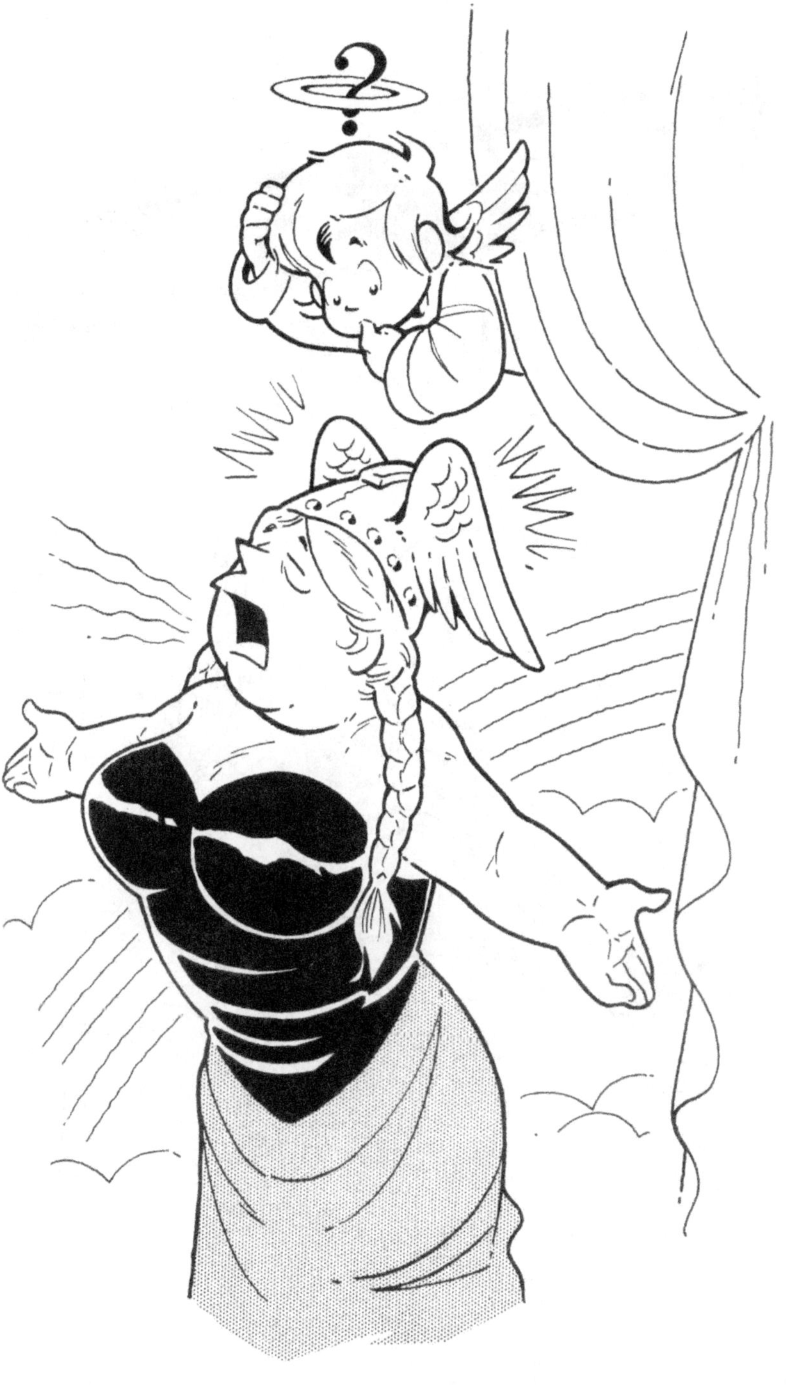

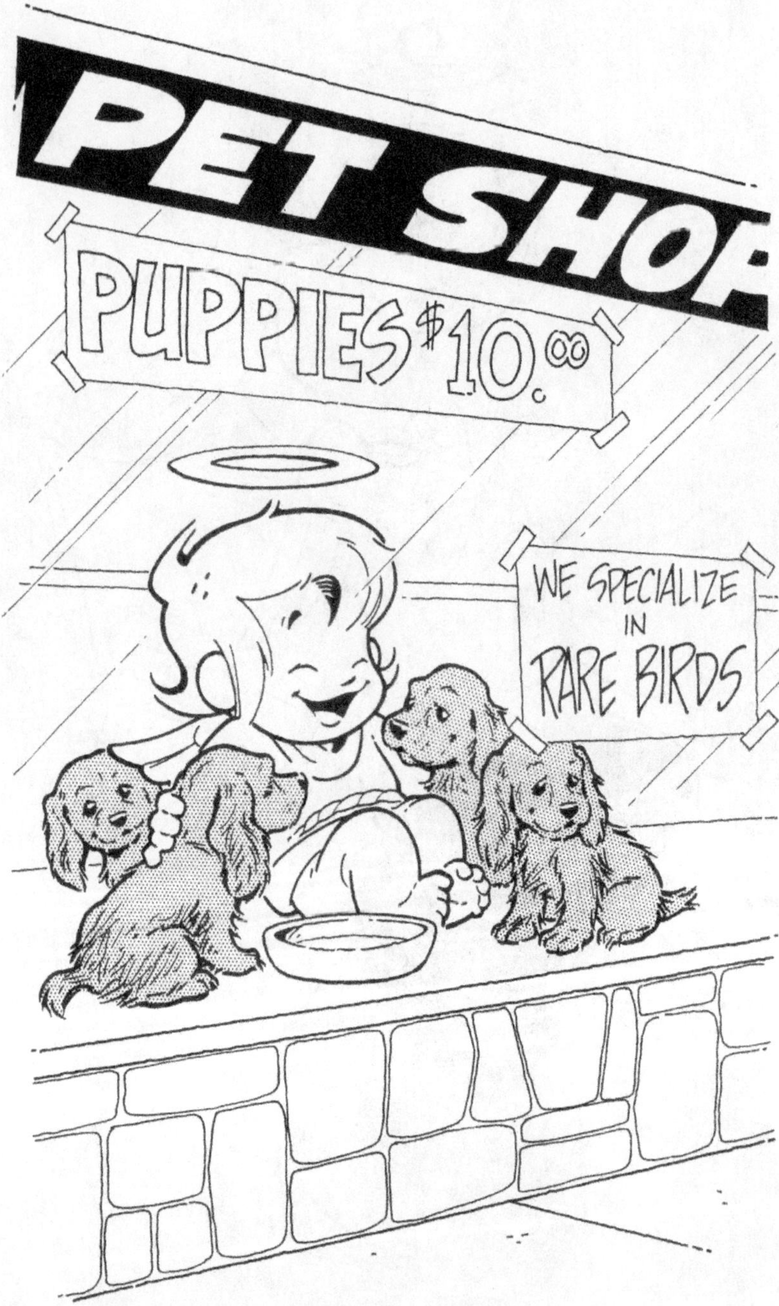
PET SHOP
PUPPIES $10.00
WE SPECIALIZE IN RARE BIRDS

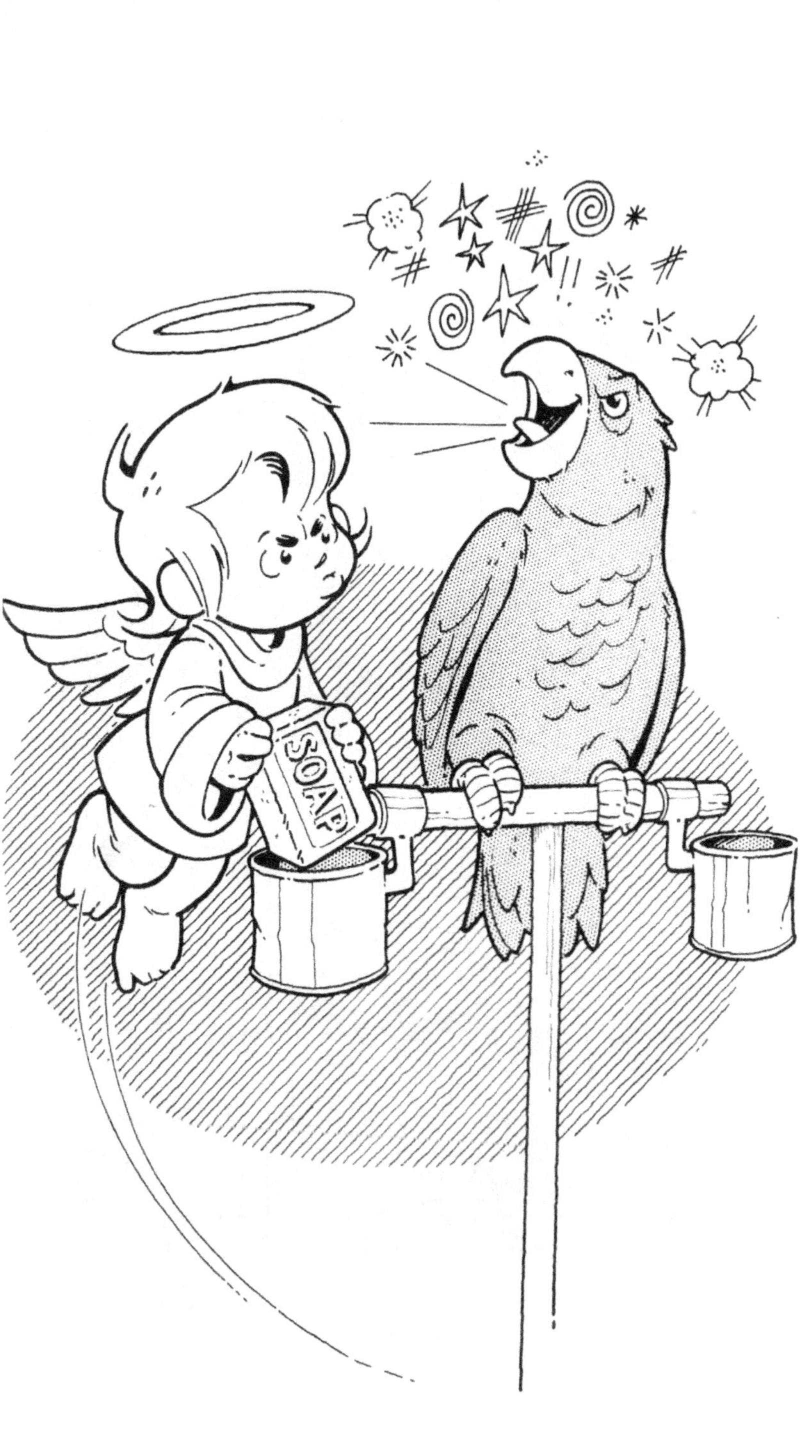
SOAP

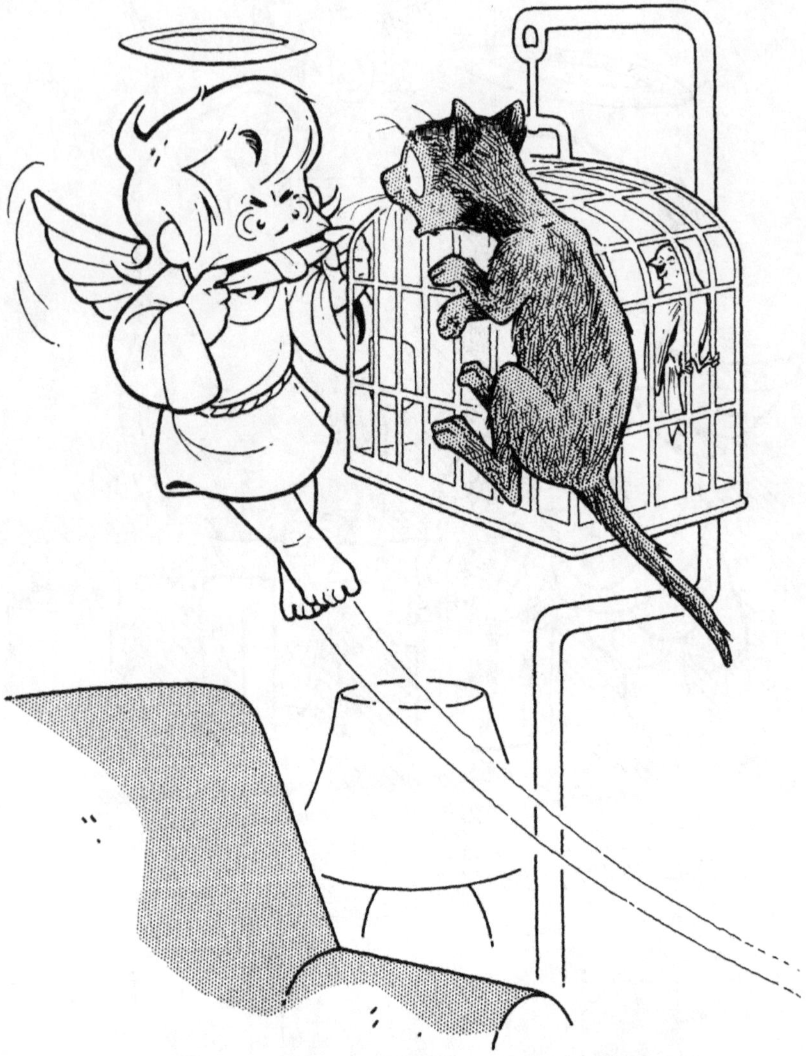

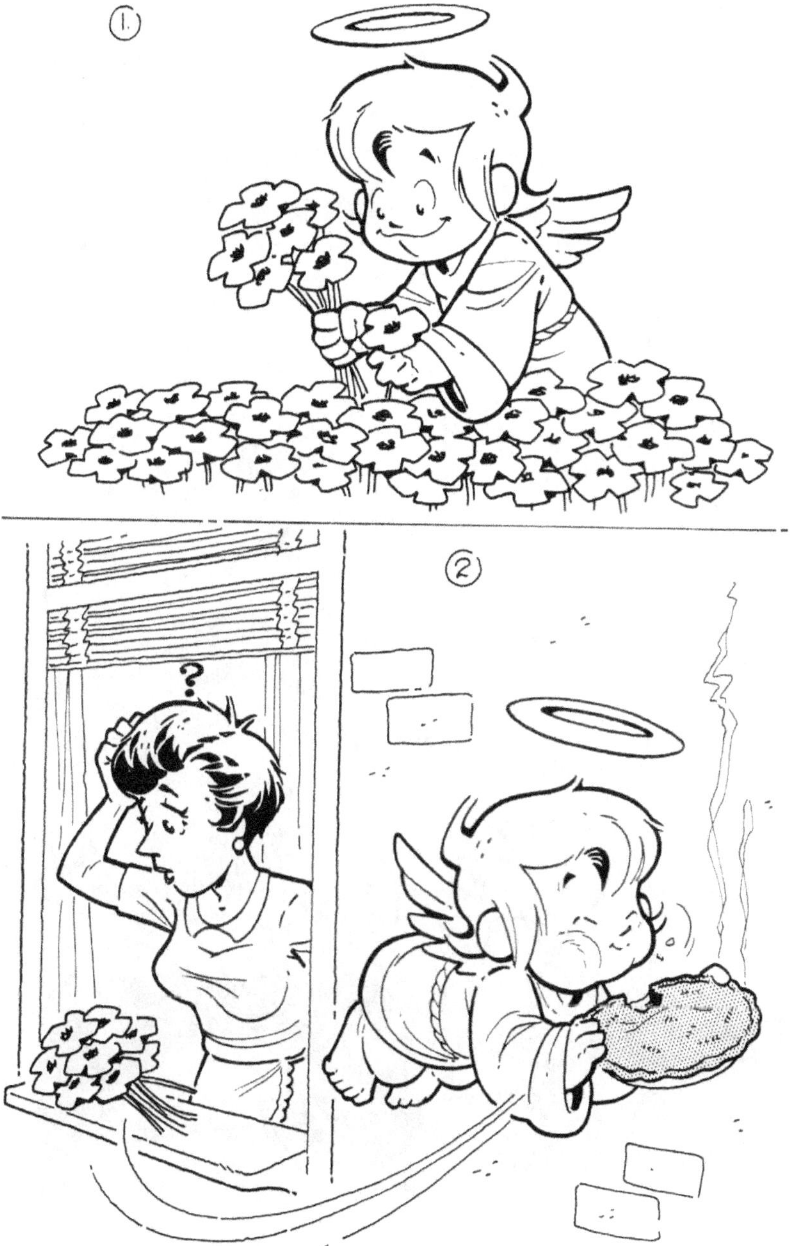

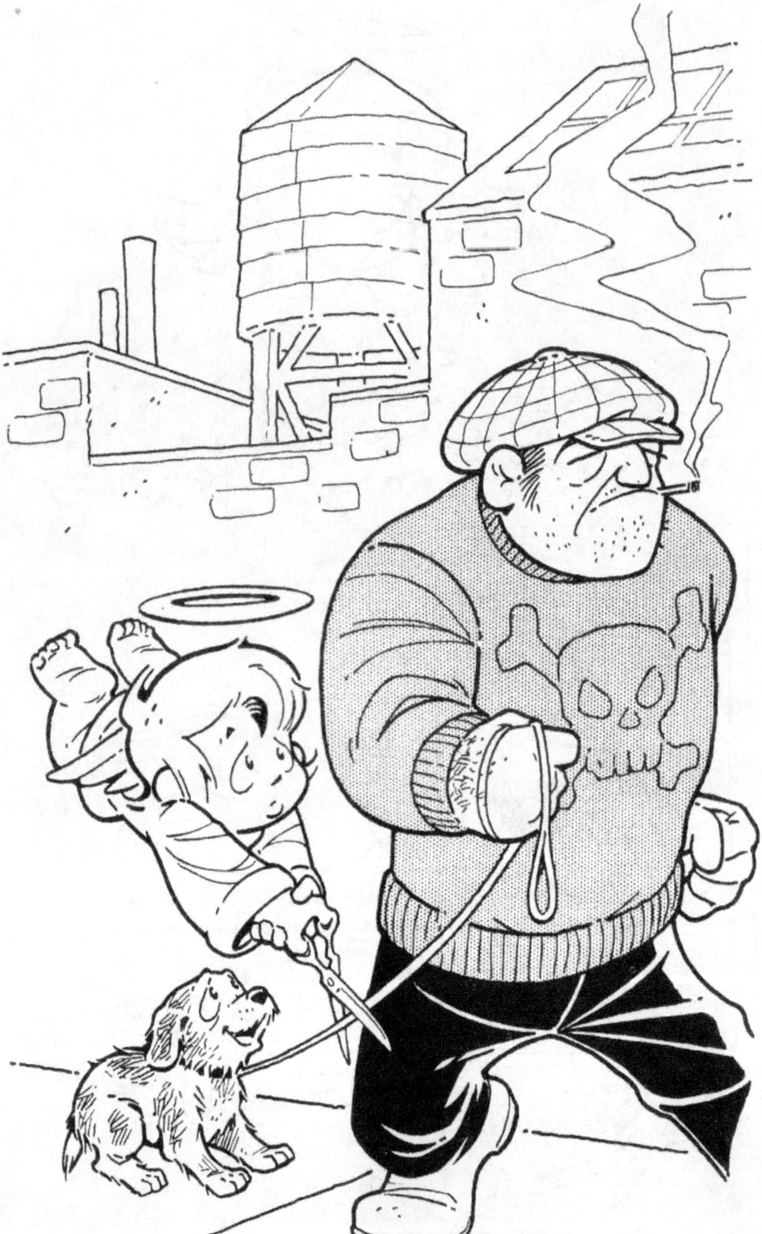

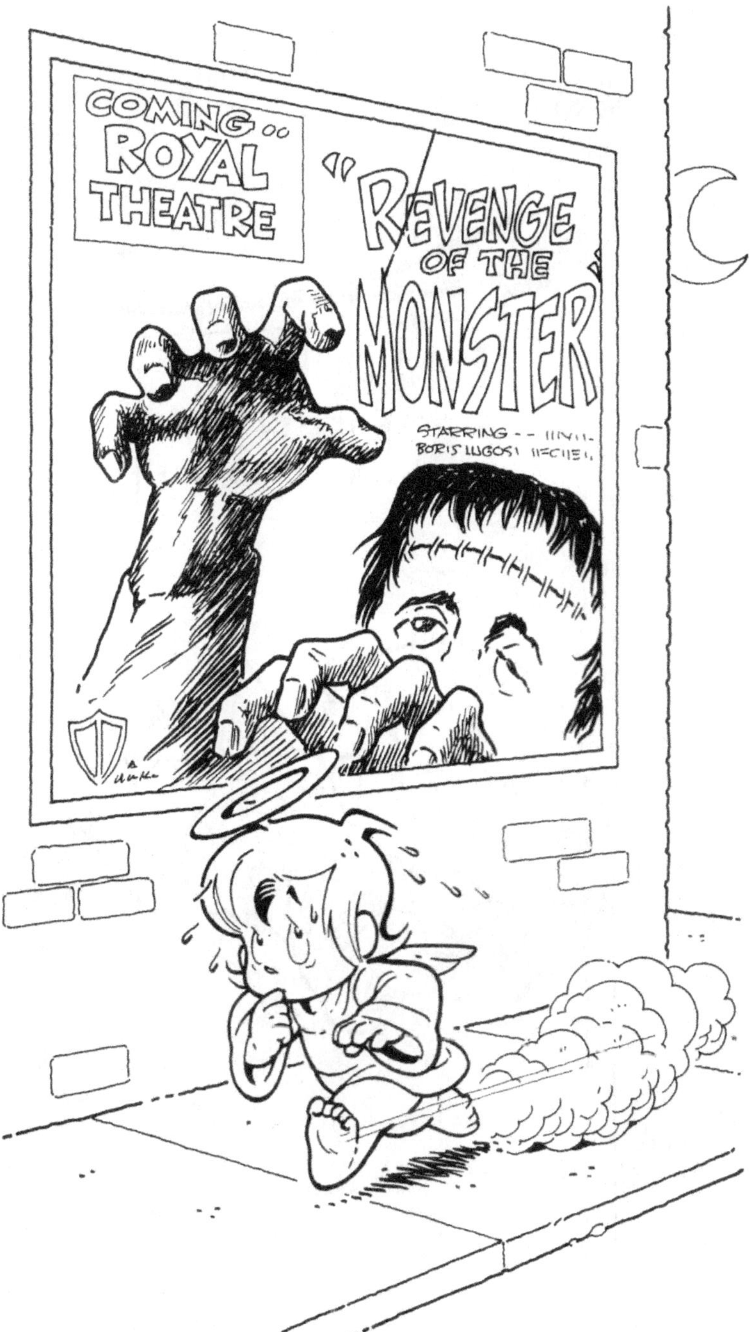
COMING...
ROYAL
THEATRE
"REVENGE
OF THE
MONSTER"
STARRING
BORIS LUGOSI

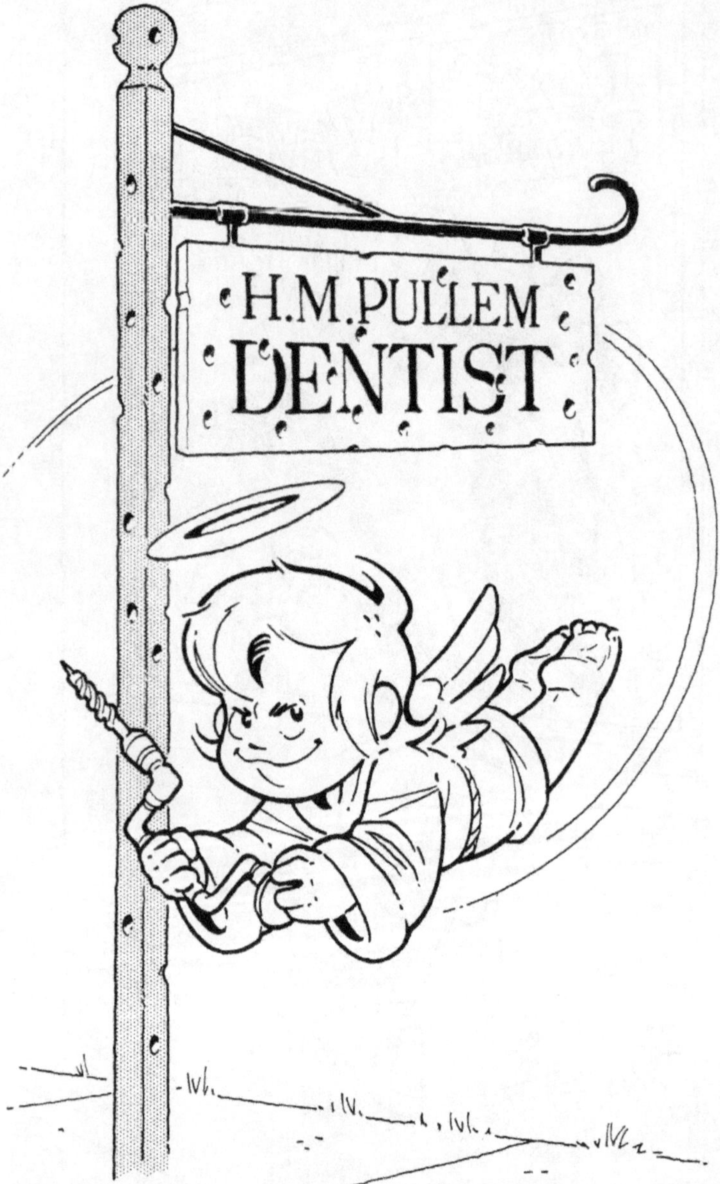
H.M. PULLEM
DENTIST

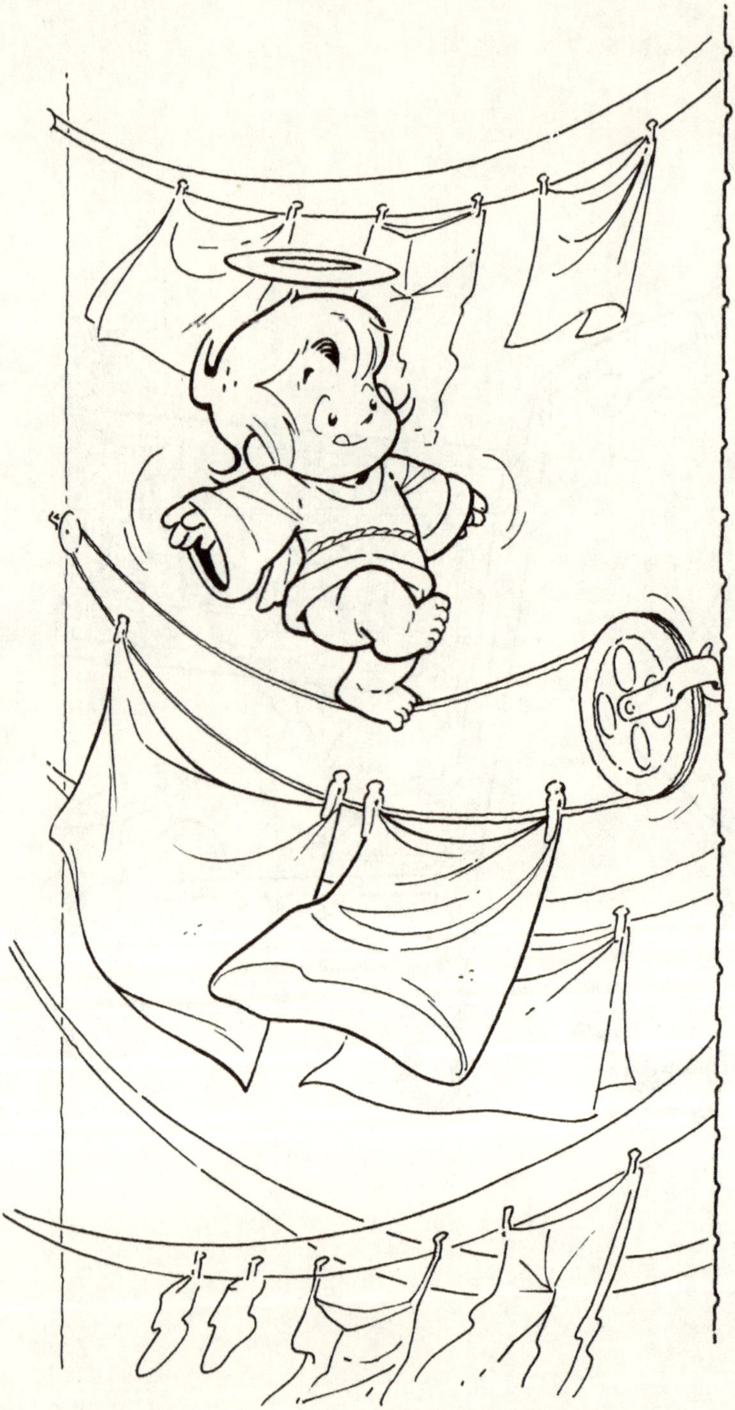

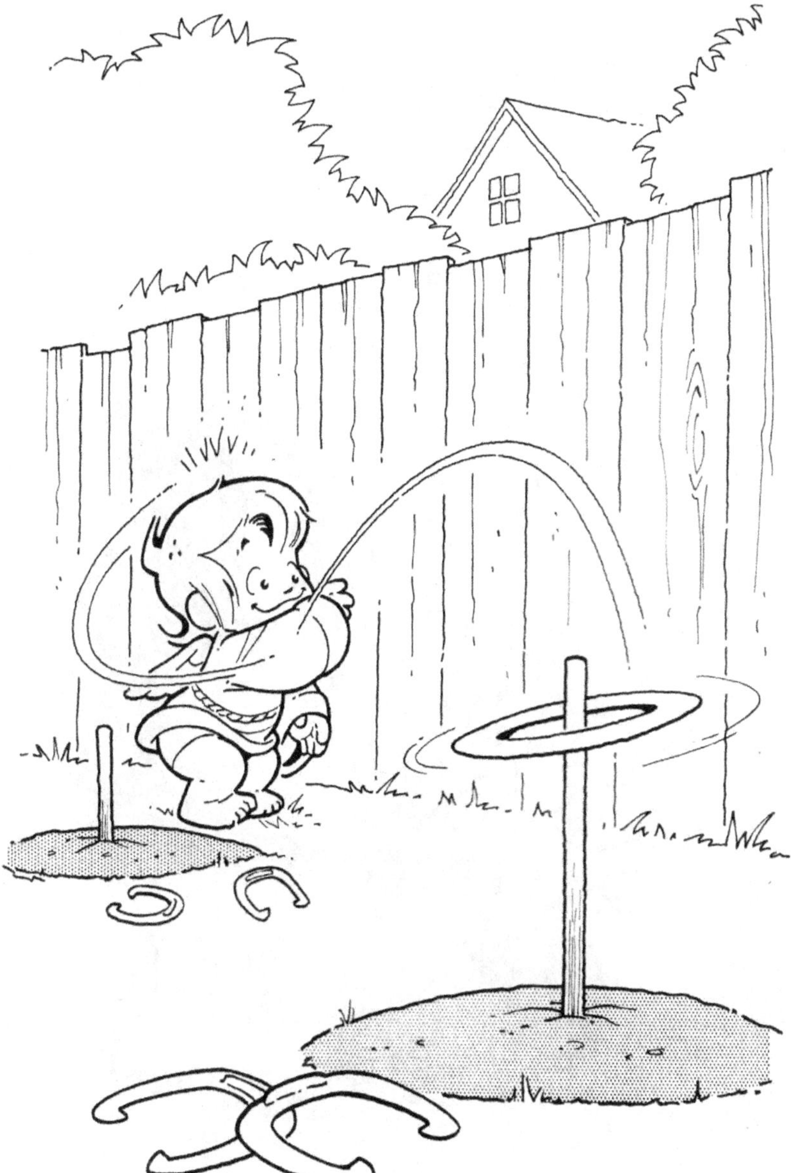

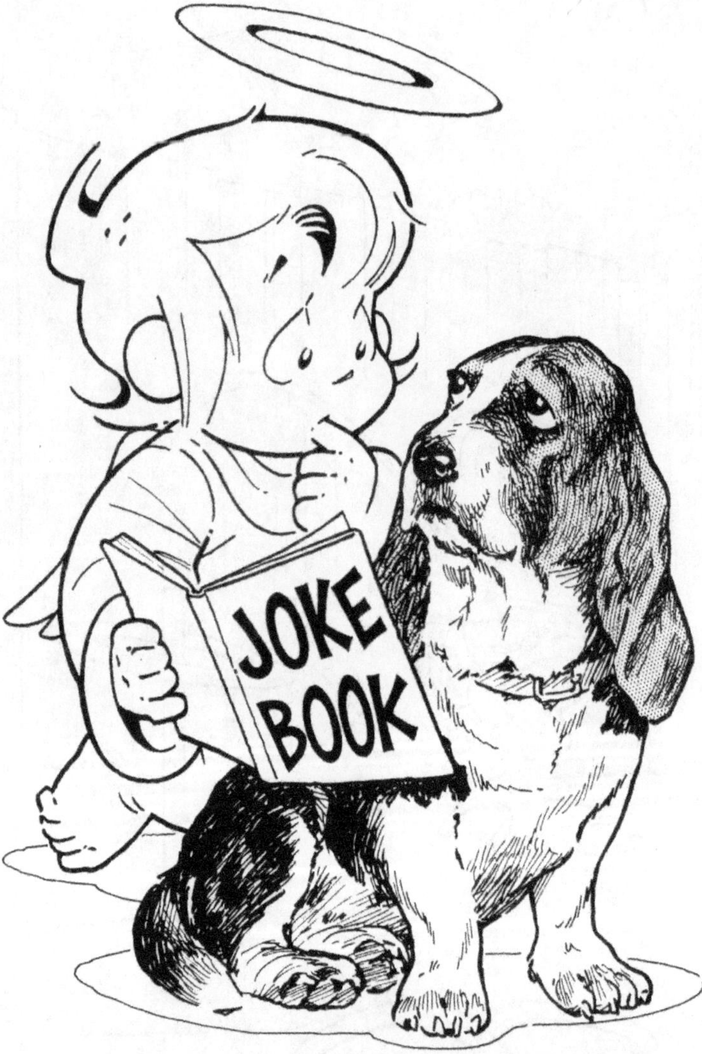
JOKE
BOOK

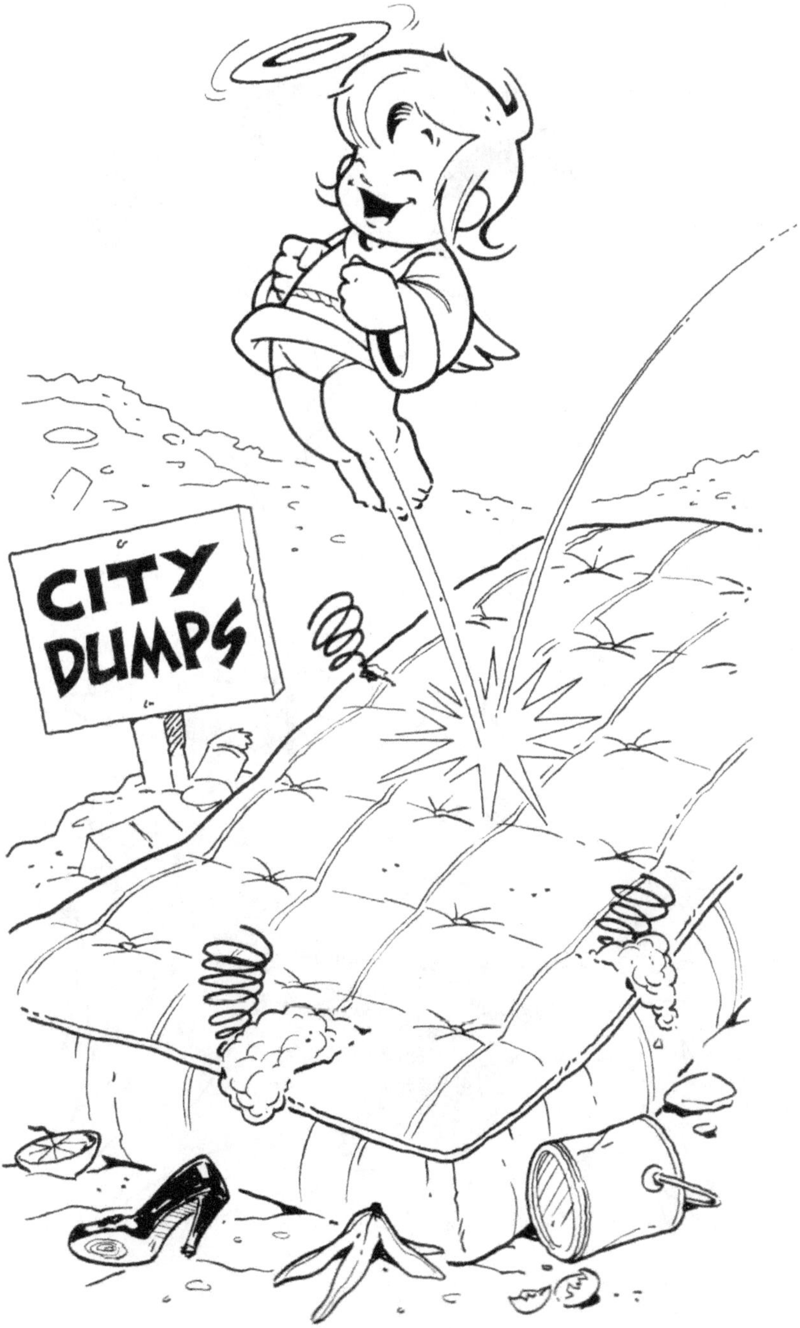
CITY
DUMPS

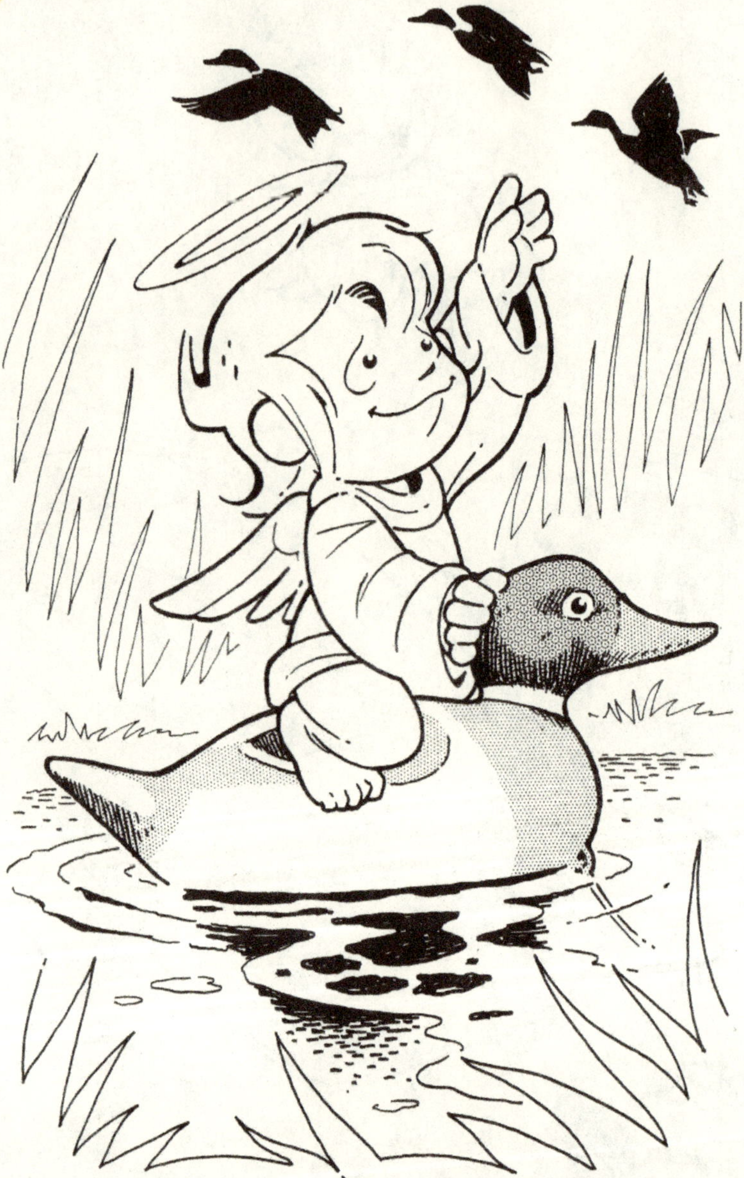

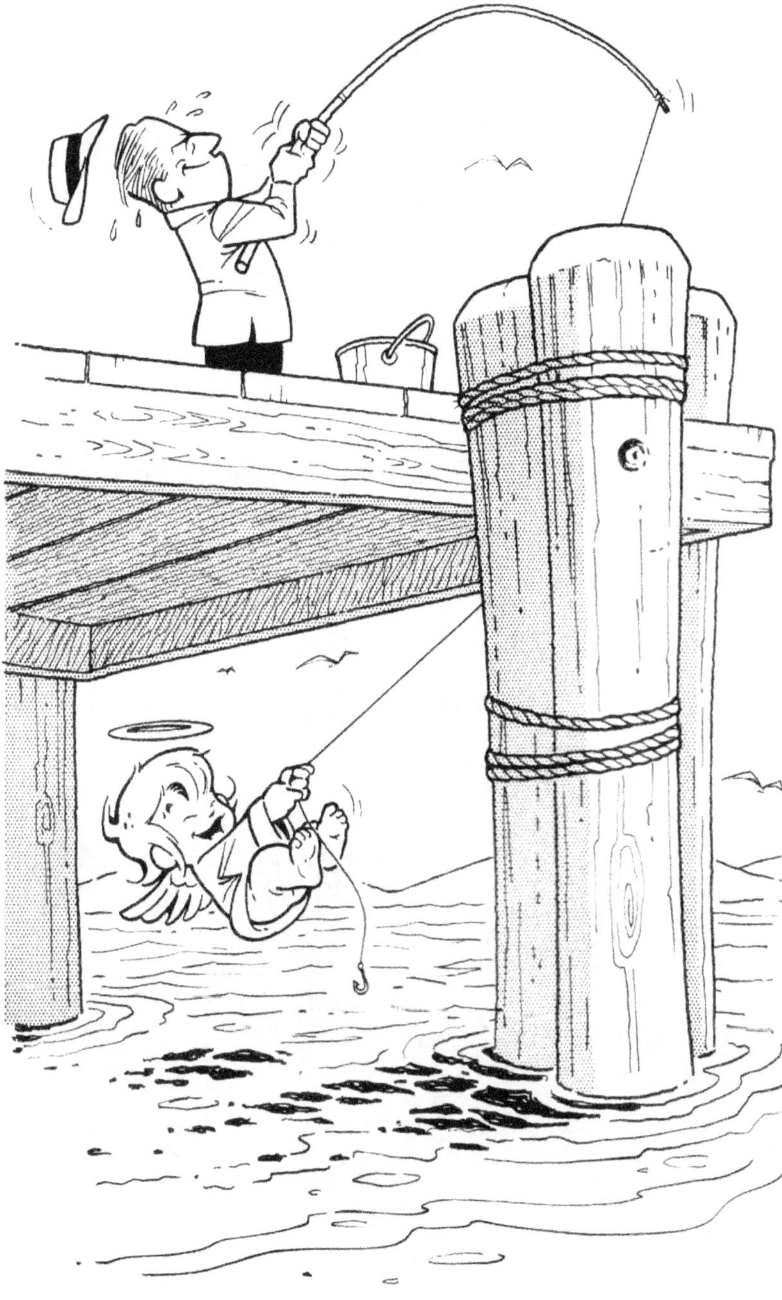

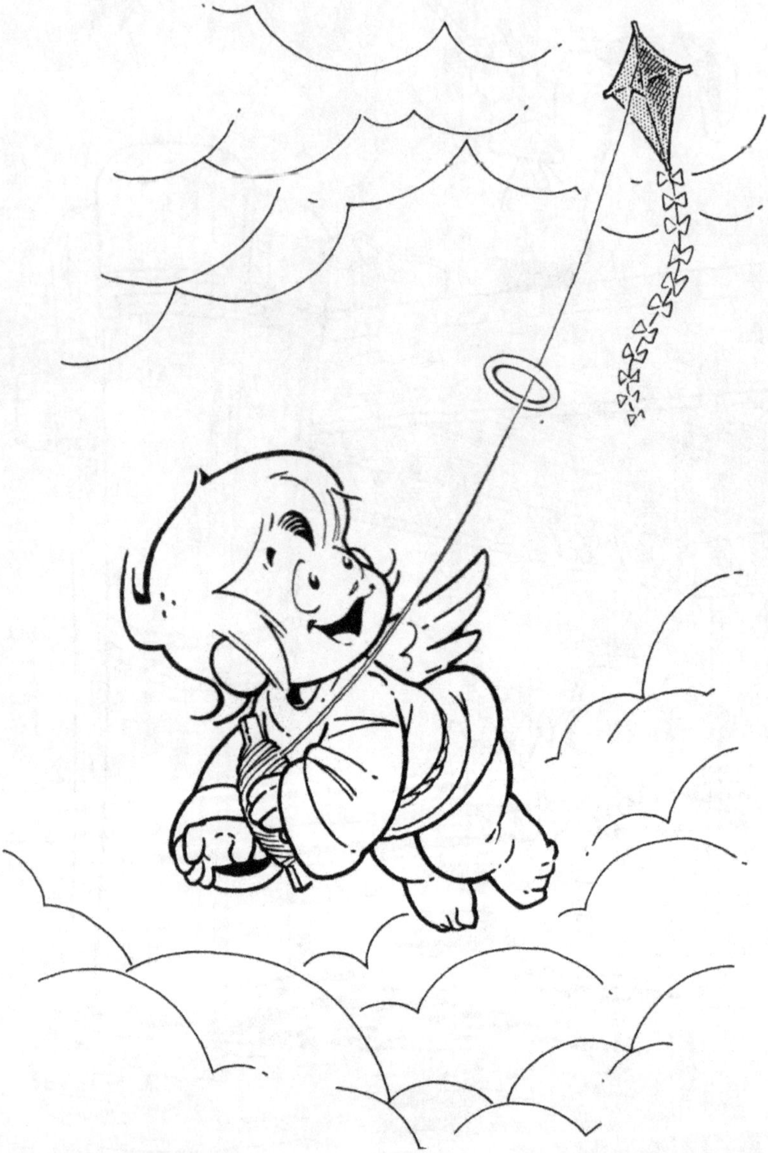

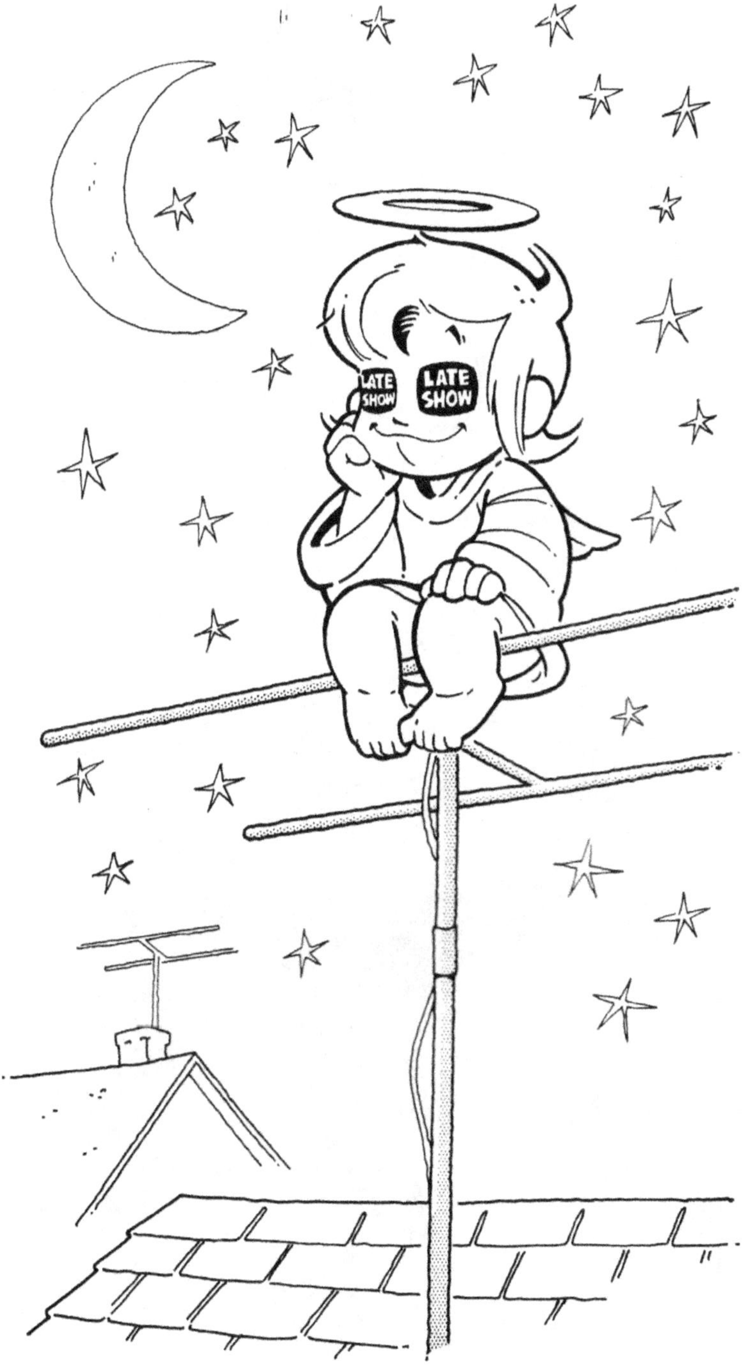
LATE SHOW
LATE SHOW

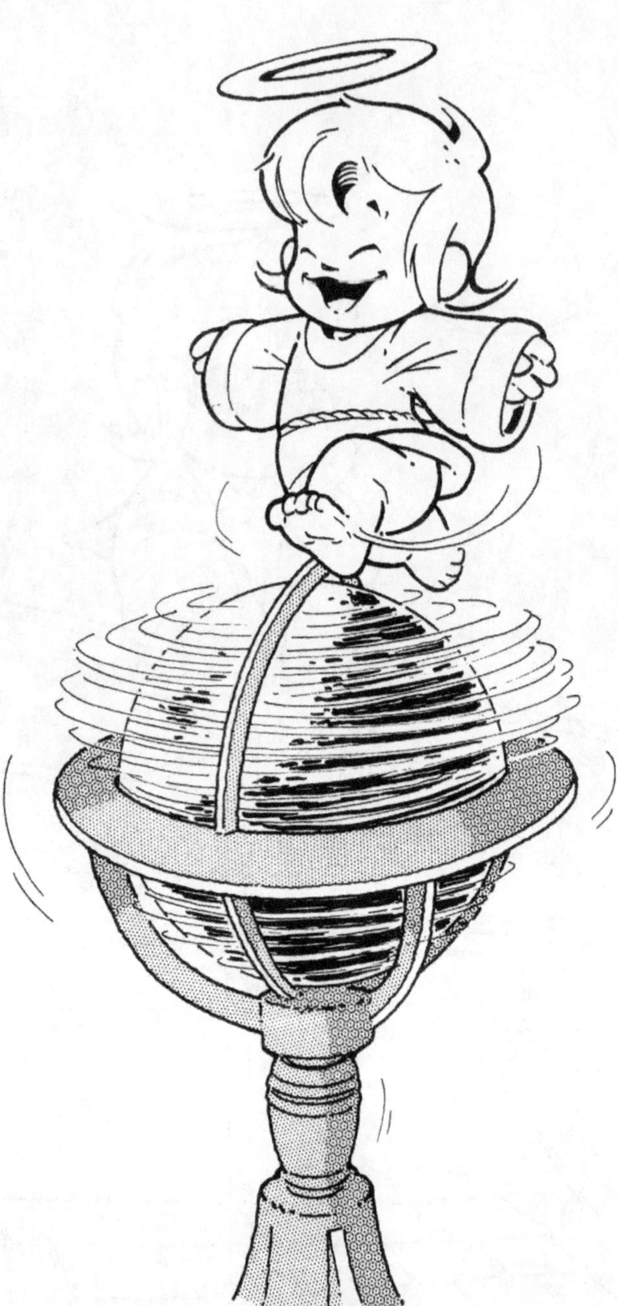

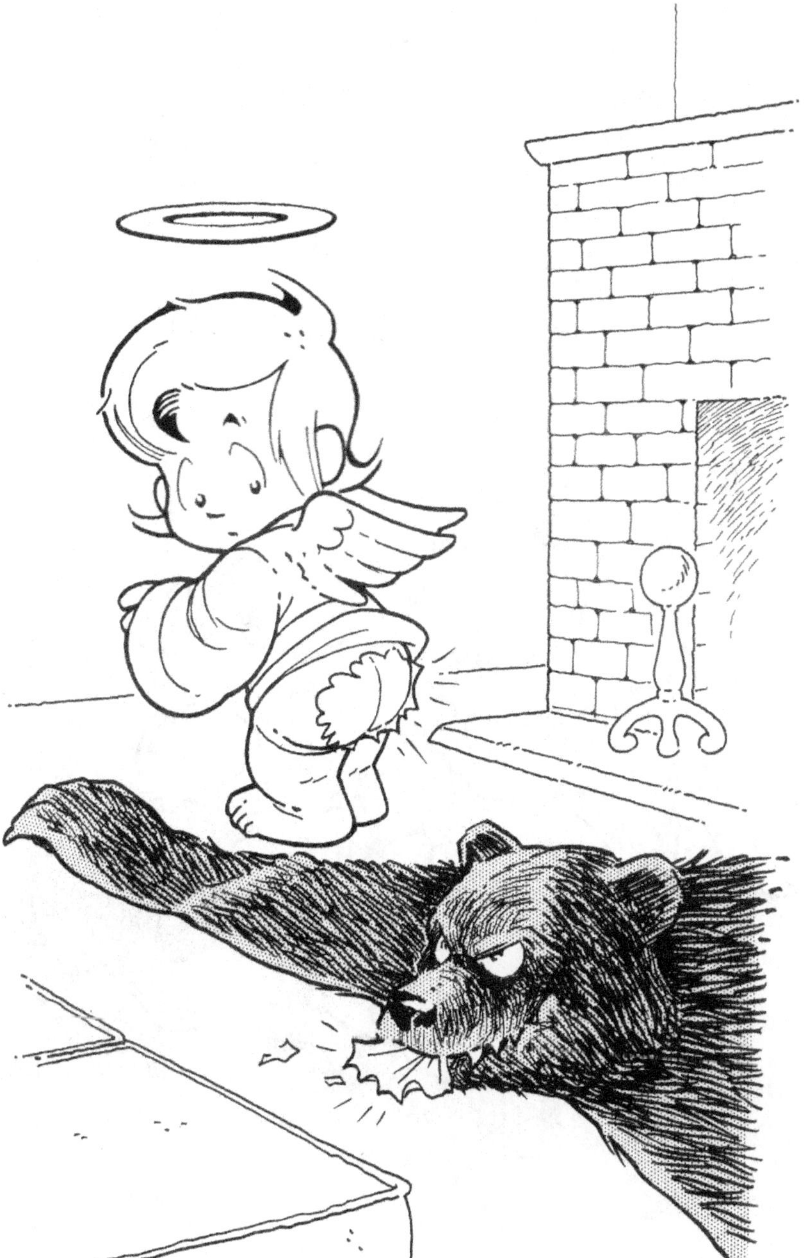

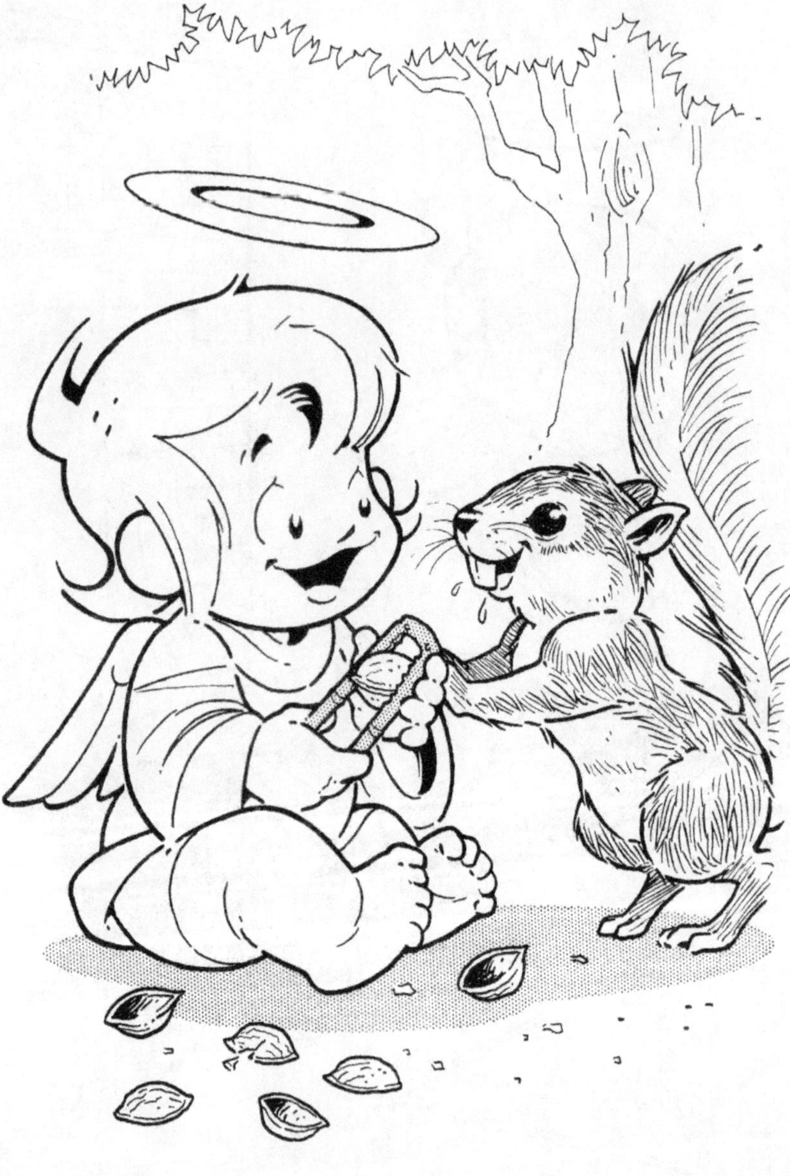

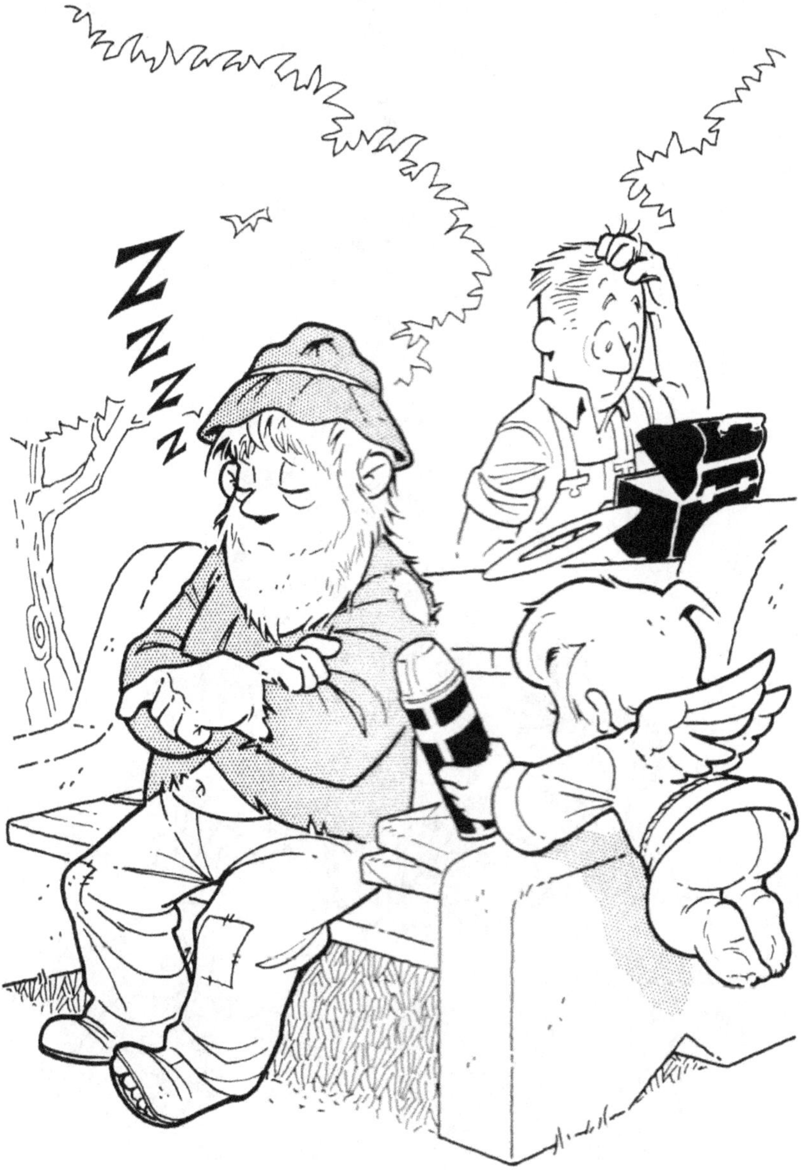

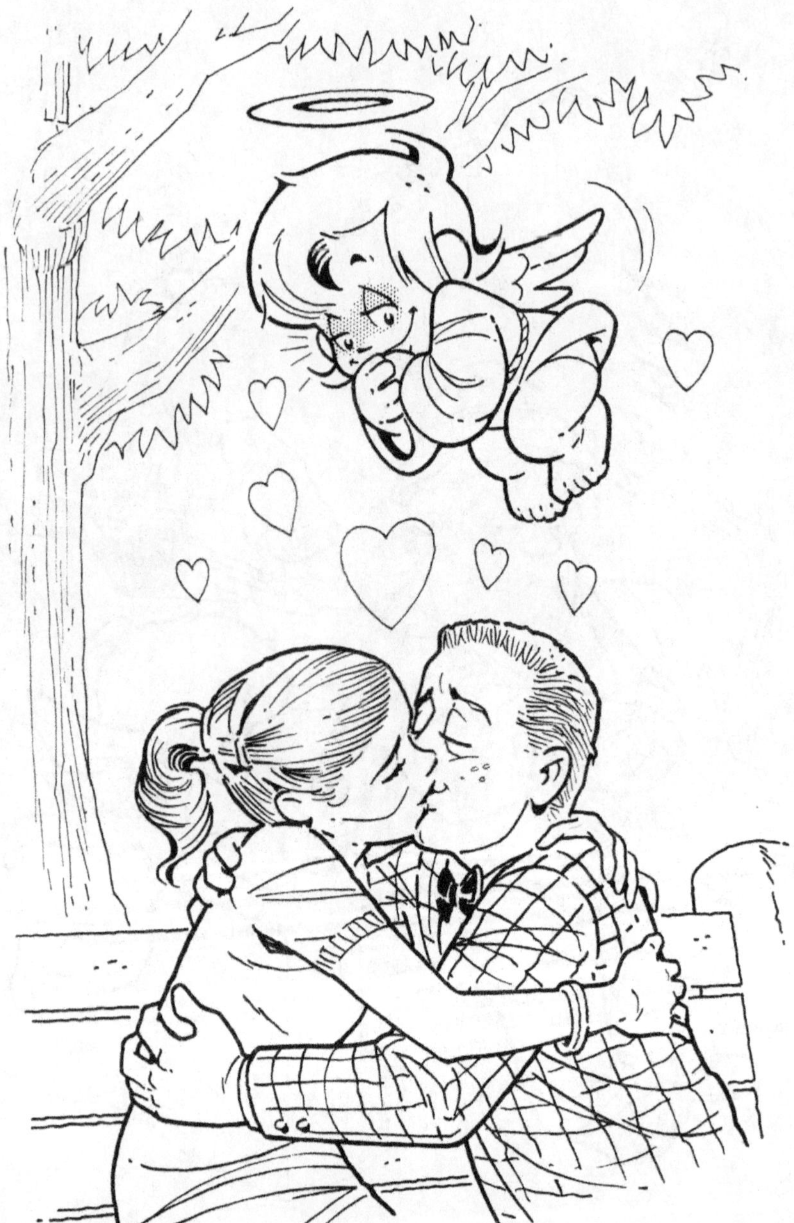

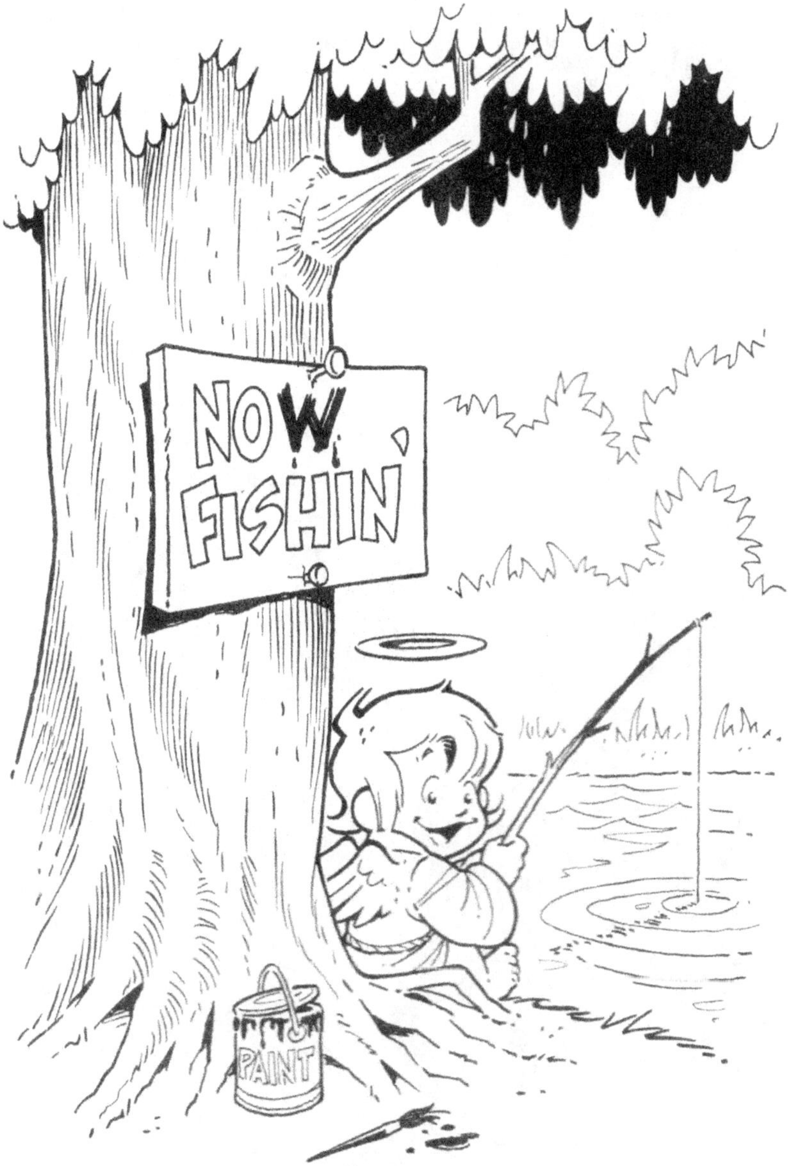
NOW FISHIN'
PAINT

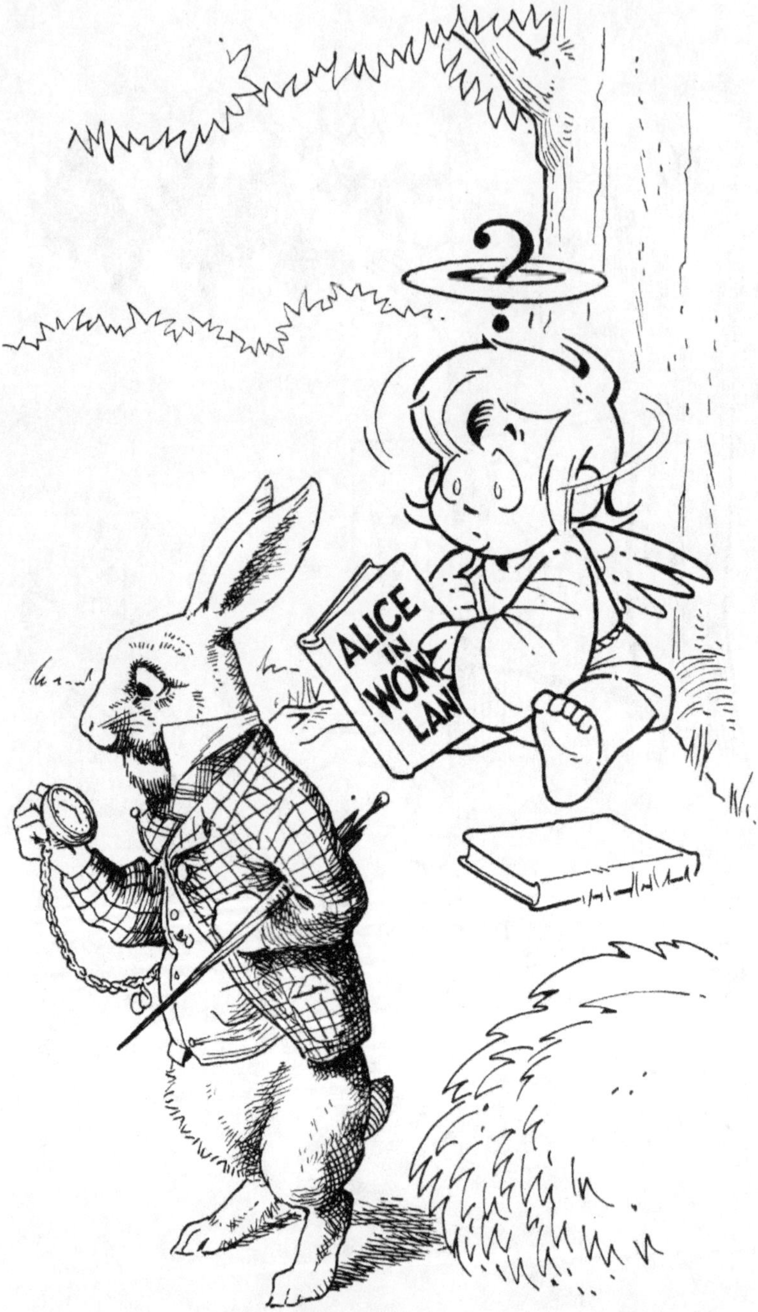
ALICE
IN
WON
LAN

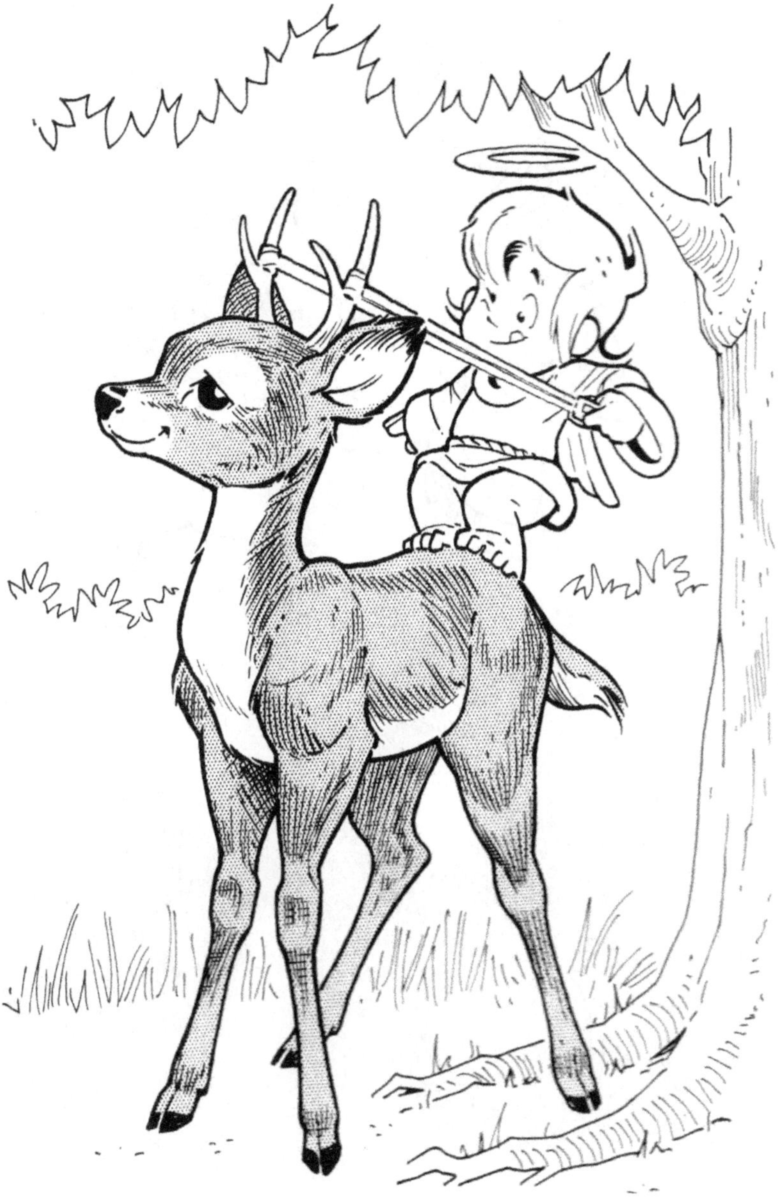

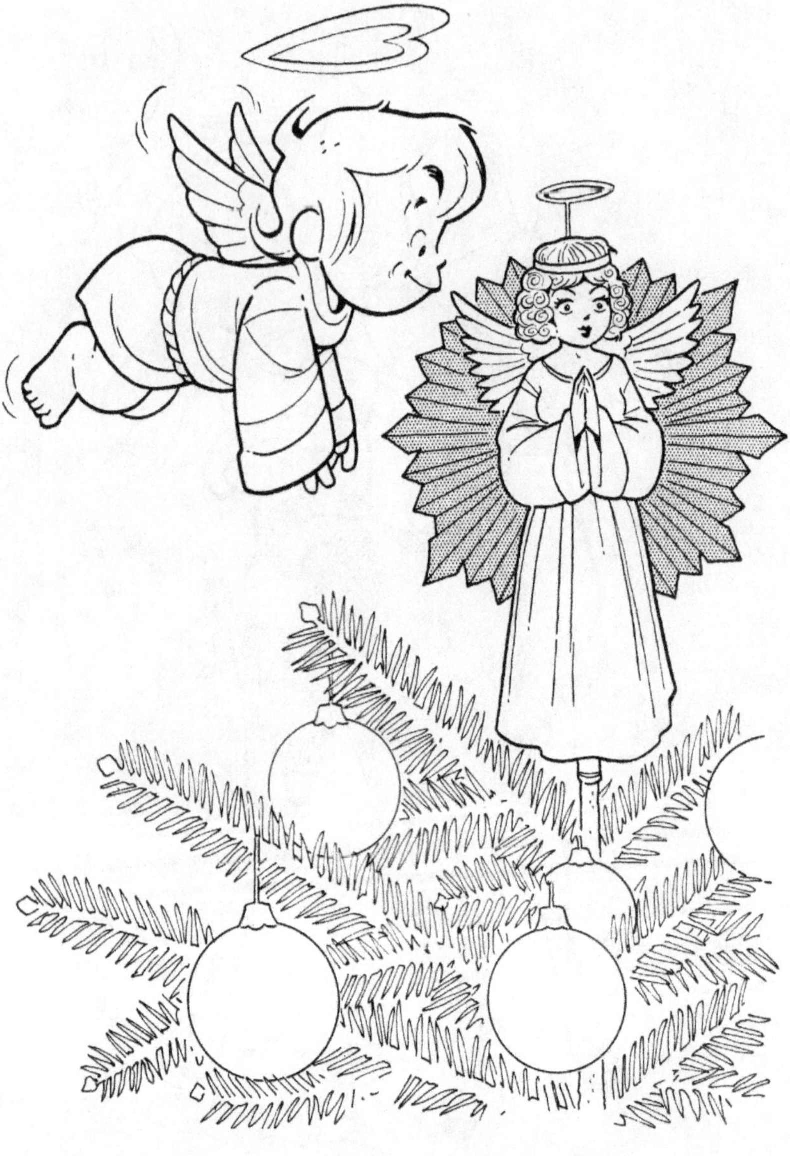

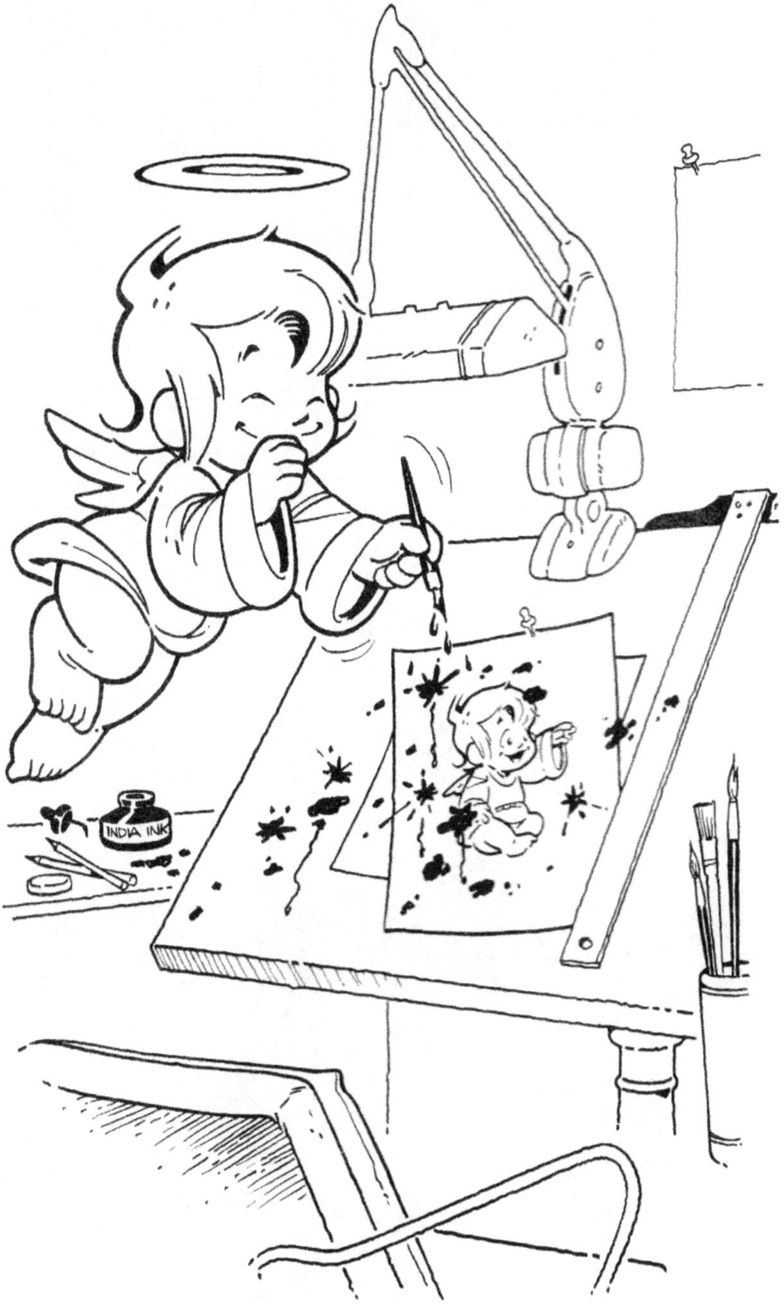
INDIA INK

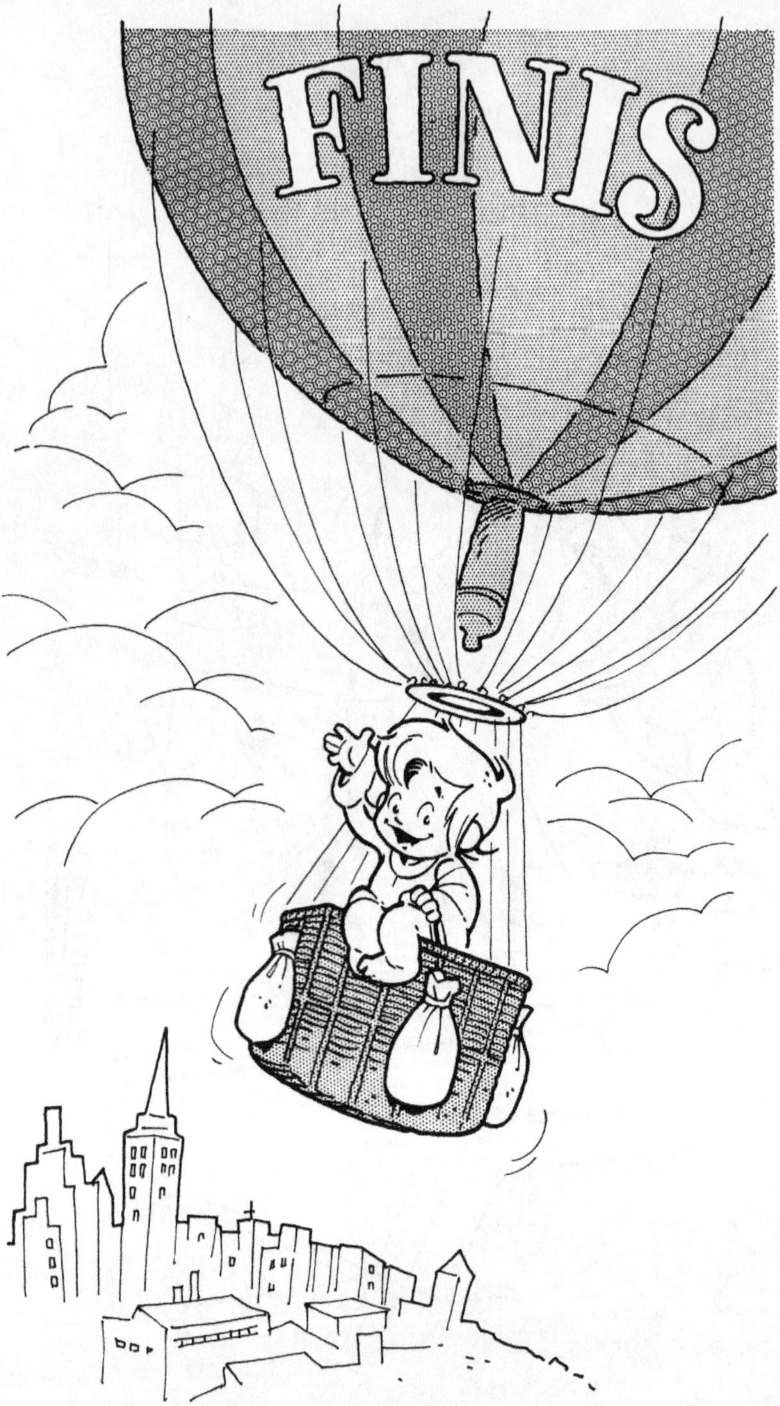
FINIS

www.ingramcontent.com/pod-product-compliance
Lightning Source LLC
Chambersburg PA
CBHW021220020426
42331CB00003B/393
9781936404919